Odyssey—The Business of Consulting

How to Build, Grow, and Transform Your Consulting Business

Odyssey—The Business of Consulting

How to Build, Grow, and Transform Your Consulting Business

Imelda K. Butler and Dr. Shayne Tracy

CRC Press
Taylor & Francis Group
Boca Raton London New York

CRC Press is an imprint of the
Taylor & Francis Group, an **informa** business

A PRODUCTIVITY PRESS BOOK

CRC Press
Taylor & Francis Group
6000 Broken Sound Parkway NW, Suite 300
Boca Raton, FL 33487-2742

Printed on acid-free paper
Version Date: 20150311

International Standard Book Number-13: 978-1-4987-2912-3 (Hardback)

Library of Congress Cataloging-in-Publication Data

Butler, Imelda K.
   Odyssey, the business of consulting : how to build, grow, and transform your consulting business / Imelda K. Butler and Dr. Shayne Tracy.
      pages cm
   Includes bibliographical references and index.
   ISBN 978-1-4987-2912-3
   1. Business consultants. 2. Consulting firms. 3. Small business--Management. I. Tracy, Shayne. II. Title.

HD69.C6B876 2016
001--dc23

2015007579

Visit the Taylor & Francis Web site at
http://www.taylorandfrancis.com

and the CRC Press Web site at
http://www.crcpress.com

In remembrance of John Butler, founder and thought leader of Odyssey: The Business of Consulting worldwide. His legacy is respected by the many professionals who have benefited from knowing him personally and learning from his teachings and practices in the "big green book," which was the original Odyssey MasterClass program.

Thank you, John, for your strategic, insightful contribution, which has made a major difference in helping so many people worldwide to fulfil their purpose in life.

Contents

Welcome from the Authors

Welcome to Odyssey: The Business of Consulting

Let me give you a brief background on how this book came about. The Odyssey concept was created in 2005 by Dave Bonnstetter, founder and CEO of Success Insights International; my husband John Butler, chairman of Century Management (who, sadly, passed away suddenly in 2010); and myself, managing director of Century Management.

Our vision, at the time, was to build a premier global consulting organization, one that would empower consultants and those who aspired to be consultants to adopt the value-driven approach to consulting and go on to build successful and highly profitable consulting businesses. Odyssey Consulting Institute was established, and in the years that followed, it became the leading global organization for enabling strategic business advantage and transformation for consultants.

Dr. Shayne Tracy from Mississauga, Canada, participated in the Odyssey process in 2010. His ethos, values, skills, and mission statement were a natural fit with everything we do at Odyssey. It was my pleasure and privilege to have Shayne join as advisor to and director of Odyssey Consulting Institute. Shayne's collaboration has strengthened our expertise, position, and drive.

Hundreds of consultants have now experienced the Odyssey process, both in peer group forums and in webinar formats, and many of these people have achieved amazing results personally and in their businesses as a result. Do not take my word for it, read what they have to say in the following pages.

Our purpose and vision, together with the masterful results that so many Odyssey consultants have achieved, continue to energize the Odyssey concept and program.

Worldwide, professional practice and consulting firms are part of a $120 billion industry, with an estimated growth rate of 16% per annum.

You only need a fraction of 1% of this market opportunity to build a successful professional services firm and to be wealthy as a partner or senior consultant.

Whatever role you fill or hat you wear in this professional world, you will need to take three steps to become a successful Odyssey Consultant:

- First, make a decision to join the top 10% of your profession—in terms of expertise, financial independence, and how you build relationships and serve your clients.
- Second, learn how to become the best you can possibly be by applying best practice and leading edge techniques and methodologies to your interventions.
- Third, make a commitment to integrate proven best practices into your business. Odyssey: The Business of Consulting offers you a process and system which can assist you in fulfilling that step.

I wish you success and happiness in the fulfilment of your purpose in life.

Imelda K. Butler

Odyssey: The Business of Consulting Is a Process Not an Event

Hundreds of people from all over the world have experienced Odyssey in one form or another over the last ten years. We have found that each person's experience with Odyssey is unique to them. But no matter what your personal journey, no matter where you start from, everyone gains value from the process. I would like to acknowledge the Odyssey graduates who committed to changing the way they run their consulting businesses. I applaud their success.

Your experience with this book will most likely start with a significant paradigm shift. As you embark on your Odyssey journey, you will begin to view your consulting "self" and how you are running your professional services business differently.

It takes time to internalize the methodologies and adopt them as your own. Nothing happens overnight. It takes dedication to continue the process of implementing the Odyssey approach over many months and years. My challenge to you is to take what you read and put it into action. You are not alone on this journey; many others like you have experienced their own Odyssey before you. A better future for you and your business lies in store.

Dr. Shayne Tracy

Acknowledgments

It is with heartfelt gratitude and appreciation that we acknowledge the many people who have made our Odyssey journey the fruitful and rewarding experience it has been. We thank you, the many unnamed persons, close to our hearts, who have journeyed with us and supported us with your friendship, expertise, and kind words of motivation along the way.

We would like to express our personal thanks to the following people for their contribution:

- Dave Bonnstetter, CEO of Success Insights International, who along with John and Imelda created the Odyssey concept and vision of an "elite consulting business" as we sat on our patio in Kildare, Ireland, in the summer of 2004.
- Bill J. Bonnstetter, who founded Target Training International in 1984 and inspired John and myself to create a consulting process and system for consultants, and who gave us access to the TTI consulting network in ninety countries worldwide.
- Rick Bowers, president of Success Insights International, who has supported the Odyssey concept and process and contributes enormously to the consulting arena internationally.
- Our Odyssey Alumni, who have contributed their wisdom and learning in their "Odyssey in Action" client case stories. We truly appreciate you sharing your journey with us, and we thank you for your warm friendship, transparency and generosity of spirit to us.
- Odyssey Alumni, who have reflected on their journeys and kindly shared their experiences with us. Thank you for being a guiding light for consultants who journey the Odyssey way in the future.

- The many consultants who have trusted the process and the concepts from the "big, green book," the webinars, the coaching, and the MasterClasses. You are indeed the heroes and heroines who learned, adapted, made the paradigm shifts, transformed yourselves and your businesses, and integrated the concepts into the success you are. Thank you for your steadfast commitment and courageous actions.
- Our clients who have participated in transformational thinking and practices with us, embraced the changes, and supported our Odyssey consultants.
- Rolando Marchis, who soldiered with us through the early stages of making Odyssey known to consultants globally. Thank you for your loyalty and support.
- Our publishers Taylor & Francis who fine-tuned and tailored the manuscript and brought this work of love to consultants worldwide. We especially thank Kristine Mednansky for her belief in us and the book, and also Ashley Weinstein for bringing it across the line in a timely manner.
- Dr. Jean Ann Larson, for your encouragement, friendship, and guidance in publishing this work and for your enlightenment along the way.
- James Flannery, who brought creative design and added the visual genius touch to the images and graphics throughout the book.
- John Hearne, our patient, dedicated editor and ghost writer who captured our thinking and concepts and scripted them into words of wisdom. You made the significant difference in producing a masterpiece. Thank you.
- Our families past and present, who have made us who we are and created the environment for us to blossom in our "sweet spots." Thank you for your support. We love you and appreciate your love for us.
- Dr. Shayne Tracy recognizes his wife Mary for her unwavering support; his three talented daughters, Megan, Erin, and Kristin, and their loving husbands, Josh, Jeremy, and Michael, respectively; and grandchildren Devon, Taya, Jordan, Tyler, Camryn and Jackson, Michael Jr., Will, and Meaghan. I am very proud of all of you. Your differences really make the difference. The world is and will be in good hands!
- Imelda K. Butler acknowledges her daughters Michelle and Maria. Thank you both for being you and for making a difference in the world by answering your callings and fulfilling your purposes. John and I are totally proud of you both, your wonderful husbands, Patrick and Geoffrey respectively, and our beautiful grandchild, Lillian, who warms our hearts and fills us with love and joy each and every day. Thank you all.

A Very Special Acknowledgment

John Butler, my *anam cara* (soul mate) and best friend who sadly passed away in 2010. You are missed dearly, but your legacy lives on in the great process you created in Odyssey: The Business of Consulting. Thank you for the joy of sharing the journey with you. Your dream of creating the legacy has come to fruition. Thank you for your vast contribution and open heart as you lived your life out loud.

Imelda K. Butler

Introduction

- What is Odyssey and how does it work?
- What is the best way to make use of this book?

The Odyssey Concept

The Odyssey is one of the two major ancient Greek epic poems (the other being *The Iliad*), attributed to the poet Homer. The poem is commonly dated between 800 and 600 BC. It is partially a sequel to *The Iliad* and concerns the events that befall the Greek hero Odysseus in his long and adventurous journey back to his native land, Ithaca, after the fall of Troy.

We chose the "Odyssey" metaphor because the quest to join the highest echelons of the consulting world mirrors many of the themes found in this, one of the oldest surviving stories in civilization.

- Spiritual growth is brought on by good times and bad times, temptations, distractions, and triumphs throughout Odysseus' ten-year journey.
- Loyalty is a major theme in *The Odyssey*. Odysseus' supporters remained devoted to him although he had been away for two decades.
- Perseverance is one of the hero's core characteristics. Despite the many seemingly insurmountable obstacles that he encounters on his journey back, he is steadfast and determined and never allows his dedication to his goal to waver.
- The importance of hospitality arises frequently in the Odyssey legend. It is what makes travel possible and gives travellers respite in a world beset by difficulties and challenges.

We are confident that the Odyssey consulting process will stimulate your quest for wisdom, truth, and knowledge, and that it will help you achieve your personal and professional purpose with passion and success.

Strategies to Manage, Grow, and Transform Your Consulting Business

Running a successful consulting practice is one of the toughest challenges in business today. Consulting is one of the fastest-growing sectors, owing to the speed of change in the corporate world and the ongoing redefinition of employment, career, and retirement criteria.

Running a consulting business differs markedly from running a conventional business. Implementing best practice consulting processes and methodologies—across business models that are constantly changing—requires special skills, abilities, and capacities along with focus and persistence to deliver masterful results.

Odyssey—The Business of Consulting is the result of twenty-five years of dedication to develop a system that gives independent consulting practices and small consulting firms the processes, methodologies, and tools to operate successfully right across the globe. The primary focus of this process is on marketing, selling, positioning, and building a profitable consulting business.

Odyssey is a journey to becoming a leading edge practitioner. It teaches you to transfer the best practice theory relevant to client needs while empowering them to solve their own problems. Odyssey strategies have prompted hundreds of business leaders and consultants alike to rethink their approach to creating business advantage.

How This Book Is Organized

Odyssey—The Business of Consulting is divided into seven chapters, each of which presents a particular aspect of the Odyssey process. These chapters build into a comprehensive exploration of the leading edge consulting system at work in the world today. Each chapter includes two or more case studies, which illustrate Odyssey in action, and concludes with a series of calls to action designed to help you benchmark Odyssey with your own business of consulting.

Chapter 1, The Consultant's Growth Path, looks at how a successful consultant builds a sustainable career and business by working through the levels and stages of the Odyssey process. We examine the four levels of the consulting model and explore a consultant's development from a variety of differing perspectives.

Chapter 2 introduces one of the most important concepts in the consultant's Odyssey. The Odyssey Arrow is a step-by-step presentation of the path to the ultimate Odyssey goal, which is to engage with your Ideal Clients on key assignments to deliver superb value and to produce masterful results. The Odyssey Arrow is the business development and value building system in the Odyssey process and provides practical guidelines for everything from attracting prospective clients through to delivering a Level 3 and Level 4 organizational intervention.

Chapter 3 examines the integration stages of the Odyssey Arrow. It continues the case study used to introduce the process in the previous chapter and reveals the series of well-defined steps and corresponding actions that allow you to manage a consulting assignment all the way through to its completion.

Chapter 4 is all about applying a client-centered value creation strategy. We examine how new techniques of consultative selling have radically altered the relationship between the client and the consultant. We also explore eight practical strategies for increasing revenues in your consulting business, discuss six different consulting perspectives, and examine ten options for intervening in the client organization.

In Chapter 5, we look at ways of assessing the metrics that govern profit, and we examine fee setting and the primacy of results-based consulting. Critically, we demonstrate how to shift your thinking to generate higher fees and drive greater profitability. Your primary aim is to generate profits to achieve the greatest possible return on your time, energy, and invested capital.

Chapter 6 explores the Odyssey consultant mind-set. We look at how you define and measure success as a professional advisor and show how to calibrate your own success in a holistic way. Harnessing the power of positive psychology is central to cultivating the Odyssey consultant mind-set. In addition, embracing personal responsibility and understanding the wider applications of the responsibility issue provide a foundation for so much of the work that successful consultants do.

Chapter 7 contains a series of reflections on the Odyssey process and how it has affected the lives and businesses of a diverse range of Odyssey graduates.

Five Tips to Get the Most Out of This Book

1. Make a decision to be the best you can be in your chosen profession.
2. Compare, evaluate, and benchmark your own current activities with topics presented in each chapter.
3. Answer the "Calls to Action" in each chapter.
4. Determine to implement three to six ideas, techniques, or strategies that are relevant for you within three days of reading.
5. Remember, action orientation is a personal leadership trait and consulting competency. Take massive and immediate action on at least one big challenge that is limiting your progress. As one of our graduates says, "Get on with it!"

Bibliography

Homer. (1912). P. G. Herbert (trans.). *The Odyssey* (Barnes & Noble Classics Series). New York: Houghton Mifflin Company.

Chapter 1

The Consultant's Growth Path

- Are you on the Odyssey consultant's growth path?
- If so, at what level are you engaging with your clients?

The consultant's growth path looks at how a successful consultant builds a sustainable career and business by working through the levels and stages of the Odyssey process. We examine the four levels and explore a consultant's development from a variety of differing perspectives, including learning, business, and communication. We also present two case studies, depicting Odyssey in action, and conclude the chapter with a series of calls to action designed to help you bring the model to bear on your own business of consulting.

Four Levels of Consulting

The model of the four parallel process levels is central to the Odyssey consulting framework (Figure 1.1). It captures the multifaceted nature of a consultant's journey while at the same time mirroring the four dimensions of the human being: the physical, the intellectual, the emotional, and the spiritual. You must attain sufficient experience and requisite skills at each level to generate the momentum to progress to the next level.

At the most basic human level, the hand does the work. The head, the center of your intellectual faculties, is responsible for thinking about the consultant role and the heart for your emotional response to it. Level 4 is the level of the soul, the most elevated plane, where the human simply "is." This highest level is about awareness and mindfulness of the present moment

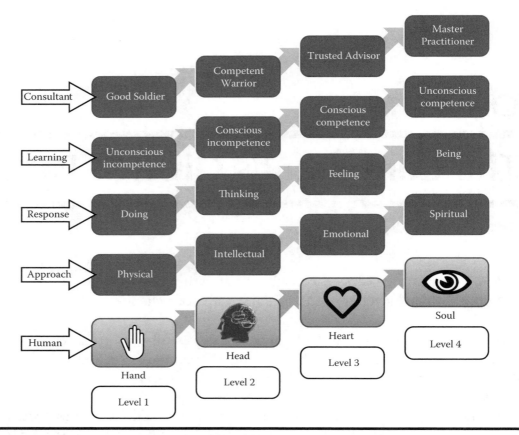

Figure 1.1 The four levels of consulting model.

and implies a radically altered mind-set beyond one engaged in simply carrying out tasks at an operational level. These gradations also mark a consultant's journey through their career.

The Good Soldier

Everyone starts out at Level 1, the Good Soldier. This is the entry level, exemplified by the enthusiastic solo professional who has just joined the profession from college or from the world of work. The barriers to entry into the sector are low; anyone can set up and call themselves a consultant. However, few stick with the pace. Fifty percent exit the profession within the first twelve months and return to corporate employment. Surveys suggest that at any one time, there are more than one million consultants working globally. These are the feast or famine years, where earnings can pitch wildly up and down and where projects undertaken tend to be based on prior work expertise. On average, a Good Soldier can earn between $50,000 and $90,000 per annum.

The Competent Warrior

Good Soldiers who remain in the business have the opportunity to become Competent Warriors. Consultants at this stage have established a track record and a reputation. You are known for being good at what you do and have built up experience together with a portfolio of solutions. Income tends to stabilize, and you begin to focus on the future and expansion. The Competent Warrior is able to generate income revenues of up to $300,000 a year depending on the client base and service level. Typically, these are short to midterm work assignments carried out at the midlevel in organizations.

The Trusted Advisor

The third level, the Trusted Advisor stage, is where consultants define their area of excellence. The Trusted Advisor refrains from selling in the traditional sense and focuses instead on adding strategic value to client solutions, blending intrinsic qualities with extrinsic ones to build mutual trust. Trusted Advisors talk about the business case and the fit of the business model for future growth. They are comfortable in the boardroom and develop peer-level respect with high-level decision makers within the client's business. The potential rewards for the Trusted Advisor are substantial.

The Master Practitioner

The Master Practitioner is the fourth and the highest competency level. It is the ultimate goal for the Odyssey professional, attained by only a small percentage of the world's consultants. Mastery of your subject can take five to seven years or more of dedicated learning and experience of the business of consulting at the highest levels. Progress towards mastery must be a mindful yet evolving process, to the point where the Master Practitioner is recognized as the subject expert or guru.

The Learning Continuum

Here, we look at the parallel process levels through several different lenses to help illustrate how a consultant's Odyssey unfolds.

The Learning Lenses

From a learning perspective, the first level is characterized by unconscious incompetence; you lack awareness even of the things you need to know. As your experience and exposure to the profession increases, you become aware of the gaps in your knowledge and you begin to ask questions: What systems do I need to invest in? What products and services work for me? How do I get clients? How do I service them? What do my clients need? You are consciously incompetent. At the third level, your experience at earlier stages gives you a base of knowledge from which you draw to expand and improve the solutions you provide to your clients; you are consciously competent. The final mastery stage of unconscious competence is when you work with ease. You are in the zone, loving what you do and doing what you love. You are answering your calling in life and fulfilling your purpose with passion and grace.

The Business Lenses

Figure 1.2 captures the consultant's career path and illustrates how each process level affects buyer type, sales activity, management, and strategy as you progress up through the four levels.

At the beginning of your career, your consulting activity consists of delivering just-in-time product-based solutions; for example, a half-day's training or an assessment. These solutions feed into the client's operational efficiency. You are managing separate events. As you progress, those events become more sophisticated and may form part of a conventional strategic intervention. The great events, however, do not begin until Level 3, where you devise innovative strategies with clients and marshal a range of interventions within that process. At Level 4, you are in collaboration with the client and operate primarily as facilitator.

At Level 1, the buyer type you deal with for your product-based transactions is almost always the end user who is likely to operate at supervisor level in the client organization. Level 2 buyers may require a little more: low-level interventions to facilitate the use of the tools you have sold. Although you are now more likely to deal with various manager levels, your solutions are still largely product based. At Levels 3 and 4, you are a solutions provider, partnering directly with the economic buyer. You are an innovator, a thought leader, facilitating the implementation of strategies that will help transform the business. This is the real business objective: to work with the

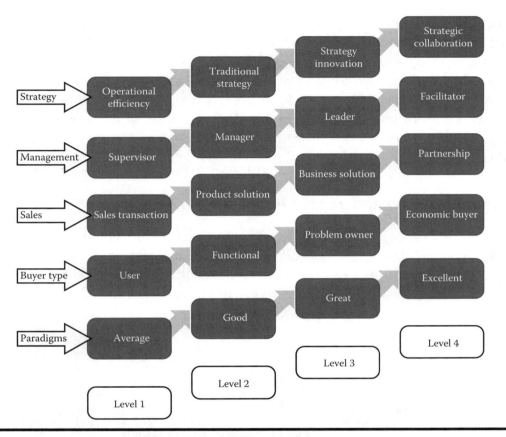

Figure 1.2 Parallel process levels with business perspective.

economic buyer in the C suite, in a position where you can make a major contribution to the entire organization and support the key visionary in leading their business forward.

At Level 4, you are in partnership with the client. There is never any question why you are there. You work collaboratively, your worth is proven, your value is recognized, and you operate at the highest level. You share in delivering value at a "big picture" level.

It is also worth pointing out that you never leave behind what you started. If you begin with a buyer type who is purchasing assessment tools from you, this can become part of your multiple revenue stream as your business evolves. However, the excitement and challenge exists in strategic innovation for major change, whether that is in a small family business or a large multinational corporation.

Remember, these levels are paradigms of thought, mind-set, and ultimately skill set; a consultant will almost always spend some time on all four levels. It is vital that you know what your percentage mix is and whether that mix is optimal for your talent and motivation. More than 80% of consultants spend most of their time on Level 1 and Level 2. Only 10% to 20% make the breakthrough to work at Level 3 and Level 4.

Archimedes said, "Give me a lever and a place to stand and I will move the world." Your leverage is determined by your position in the parallel process model, and position is everything in creating personal and consulting advantage.

Communication and Team/Organization Dynamics

The parallel process levels also help illustrate how teams come together and communicate (Figure 1.3). This process must be internalized by a consultant as it is very helpful in assessing team and executive dynamics in the context of providing solutions for corporate growth and expansion.

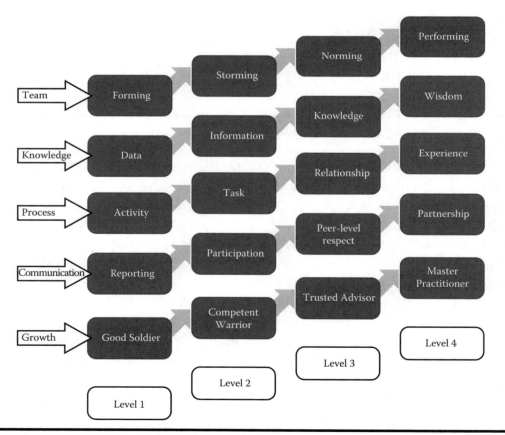

Figure 1.3   Communication and team/organization dynamics.

Team members at the forming stage are getting to know one another before embarking on a new adventure, a process that is often accompanied by a certain level of enthusiasm and heightened expectations. The reality of course is that not everyone sees things the same way; differences in outlook may often surface. Then comes the storming stage when these differences become potentially divisive. Team conflicts must be worked out and processed to get to a point where members are able to accept, process, and understand one another's perspectives and contribution. This is the norming stage. Having achieved this cohesion, the team arrives at a point where it can deliver "exceptional collective performance" (ECP): the performing stage. This is a stage where the consultant is the team leader or facilitator, where roles and objectives are clear, results are achieved, and rewards are shared appropriately.

Think of a football or a hockey team. You are excited to be picked, but now there's the drudgery and discipline of preseason training. It is only when you persevere through this phase that the process of doing what needs to be done and working together as a team becomes the norm. By following the discipline of working well together, the team gels and is able to perform effectively in the game (ECP) and go on to win.

You will also experience the forming, storming, norming, and performing dynamics on an individual level as you grow your business.

In the knowledge stream, consultants at Levels 1 and 2 concern themselves primarily with the raw data and information that comprise the kinds of low-level intervention associated with the Good Soldier and Competent Warrior. The integration of experience, mind-set, and emotional intelligence gives the Trusted Advisor the funded wisdom to operate at higher levels, developing peer-level respect with clients to produce exceptional results. As a Trusted Advisor and Master Practitioner, you develop strong relationships that enable the C-level client to partner with you in high value interventions and solutions.

The communication stream follows the same path. At Level 1, the Good Soldier is concerned with low-level consulting interventions such as report delivery. There is participation at the second stage where the two-way flow of information between consultant and client begins. At Level 3, the consultant arrives at a thorough understanding of the client's objectives through dialogue and rapport, which generates peer-level respect. At the mastery stage, the Odyssey consultant is working in partnership with the client on a long-term basis, in a climate of undisputed trust.

Communications is to a relationship as blood is to the body. Without either, there is no life. Communication is therefore imperative to the development of strong business relationships.

The Consulting Levels in Detail

We characterize the Level 1 consultant as the Good Soldier (Table 1.1). Your consulting output is transactional in nature; you sell directly to the end user who needs the product to meet immediate work needs. At this early stage of your career, you are unaware of what you need to learn, and so you are unconsciously incompetent. Sometimes we refer to it as the "arrogance of ignorance"; you do not know that you do not know. In the human dimension, this stage is represented by the hand.

At Level 1, you are hands-on and transaction orientated, as are the buyers you tend to deal with. They are not looking for business solutions, and they are not positioned to see the big picture. They want a day's training or some coaching. They want 80 assessments for a team building exercise. The work you do is time bound and off the shelf and only seeks to improve operational efficiency in that specific area. The way you think and work tends to be short term.

Life as a Good Soldier

When my husband John and I started in business, we were Good Soldiers. We set up our company in March 1989 with one product, a business management course. We named our company Century Management because we were relatively young at the time and wanted to appear substantial and long-established.

We planned to blossom where we were planted. Living in Kildare, Ireland, we approached our local businesses—the butcher, the baker, the

Table 1.1   The Good Soldier

The Level 1 Consultant: The Good Soldier	
Step 1	*Physical*
Consultant growth stage	The Good Soldier
Buyer type	User of a product
Market positioning	Transactional sale
Needs analysis	Work needs
Learning stage	Unconscious incompetent
Human dimension	Hands/physical

accountant, the solicitor, and the local small- and medium-sized business owners—the people who would not be inclined to go to the corporate houses for training. And our vision worked. We began to develop a loyal and happy local client base.

At that stage, we were running the business from our converted garage. Our main objective was to fill the Business Management Competency Course (BMCC), which we had created. The BMCC program comprised several business modules that were relevant, practical, and results orientated for small- to medium-sized businesses.

Having the helicopter view into many businesses and helping them solve their problems and achieve their visions suited our style and work. We loved working with a varied clientele. This perspective enabled us to develop a strong reputation for making a difference for people in both their personal and business lives.

We may have been short on experience, but we were certainly big on ambition, and that's typical of most consultants at this stage of their development. They arrive into the profession from either technical or general management with high hopes and vigor. The scope of the consulting business is a breath of fresh air after the limitations of management, and this fuels a passion and a sense of freedom. Very often, however, consultants throw themselves into activities with limited success or results. The Good Soldier years are always a mix of excitement and struggle.

Level 2 consultants are Competent Warriors (Table 1.2). They sell their product-based solutions to functional managers with a particular product requirement. They are now aware of the gaps in their skill sets and are consciously incompetent. This is what's sometimes referred to as the

Table 1.2 The Competent Warrior

The Level 2 Consultant: The Competent Warrior	
Step 2	*Intellectual*
Consultant growth stage	The Competent Warrior
Buyer type	The functional manager
Market positioning	Product solutions
Needs analysis	Product needs
Learning stage	Conscious incompetent
Human dimension	Head/intellectual

"embarrassment of exposure"; you know you do not know. The human dimension is the intellectual component, the head.

Kicking It Up a Level

John and I knew that we had to move our offering up a level. We had to source resources to advance us from the feast or famine cycle, to give us something more than just the one product. During the Competent Warrior years, the consultant who wants to "kick it up a level" puts their management and business hat on. They look beyond their own services and explore collaboration and partnerships with other professional consultants.

We decided to connect with a renowned global expert, Brian Tracy, who provided us with the resources and the brand to expand our offering. We partnered with Brian and incorporated his materials into our portfolio of solutions.

We also formed a relationship and business partnership with Bill and Dave Bonnstetter at Target Training International and Success Insights (TTISI). Bill and Dave continue to research and add world-class innovative systems to the world's leading assessment solutions in business diagnostics, job competency and measurement, personal talent, and behavioral and motivator systems. They were the first organization worldwide to computerize temperament/behavioral profiles.

Since we had been handwriting our behavioral reports up to this point, their materials transformed much of what we did. Similarly, their software and know-how revolutionized our systems and made the reports we presented to clients far more professional.

We were no longer one-dimensional. We had what we could legitimately call a portfolio of solutions. We were also able to license out our business training programs to other consultants, which helped to widen our revenue base and smooth the troughs and peaks that tend to dog those early years.

We had broken out of the Good Soldier stage and become Competent Warriors. Consultants at this stage of their career tend to have an established track record and reputation. You are known for being good at what you do, and any innovations you make start to bear fruit. You still get lean periods, but you have survived the early years and adding to your portfolio gives you breadth and depth. It is at this point that people typically think about hiring an additional consultant, an administrator, and move—as we did—from the garage to professional, purpose-built offices.

You are still in the product business, but there has been a subtle shift in how you think about yourself and your clients. You are out prospecting,

Table 1.3   The Trusted Advisor

The Level 3 Consultant: The Trusted Advisor	
Step 3	*Emotional*
Consultant growth stage	The Trusted Advisor
Buyer type	The owner of the problem
Market positioning	Business solutions
Needs analysis	Performance issues
Learning stage	Conscious competent
Human dimension	Heart/emotional

trying to develop a good pipeline. You are getting to know what your clients want, and it is that growing awareness that you will use as a springboard into the next stage. You develop marketing strategies. You begin to see the impact your service portfolio is having on clients, and you also begin to see the potential for leveraging those solutions deeper into the client organization.

Trusted Advisors operate at Level 3 (Table 1.3). They have graduated to partnering with the client/owner of the business problem and generate business solutions that address the performance issues their clients face. They have developed a knowledge and methodology base from which they draw to service their clients' needs. They are now consciously competent. This is the "awkwardness of awareness" stage; you know you know. The human dimension for the Trusted Advisor is the heart.

Thinking Like Business People

Throughout the Good Soldier and Competent Warrior years, we were thinking like sales people. We now needed to think like business people. There was an obvious, logical fit there. We were searching for ways to grow our business, and so too were our clients. Selling them a training course or an approach to personal development alone was not going to do that.

Moving to the Level 3 Trusted Advisor stage is a massive step, one that fewer than 20% of consultants ever take. Although those at soldier and warrior stages do good work delivering ad hoc consulting assignments and very clearly defined projects, the work of the Trusted Advisor is very different.

You stop talking about the features and benefits of your products, and you talk about the client's profits, the client's return on investment. You move away from a transaction-based approach, and you begin to see how your personal knowledge bank, expertise, and talent can add value to your client's business.

Increasingly, your point of contact in the organization is the economic buyer. You shift onto the CEO's wavelength, and your unique offering becomes embedded in the client company's objectives. Your perspective widens; the discreet interventions you once sold are now supplanted by strategies that engage the client's entire business.

Trusted Advisors talk about results, performance, and business solutions. They are comfortable at senior executive and at board level. Trusted Advisors do vital work for niche markets, with clients that are loyal to them and vice versa. They have gone beyond the feast or famine roller coaster, and they enjoy what they do and work primarily with their Ideal Clients.

"Who is the owner of the problem at a strategic level?" is a key question. What is the problem? How well is it defined? Why hasn't it been solved already? The "already" question can uncover the real source of the challenge.

As a Trusted Advisor, your cost becomes irrelevant because it will be miniscule compared with the added value your client receives if you can solve their problem or help implement the change they seek.

At Level 4, Master Practitioners deal directly with the economic buyer at the summit of the client organization (Table 1.4). They are in strategic partnership and work to meet the client's strategic wants. At this level—with the soul providing the mirroring human dimension—the consultant is unconsciously competent. This is the "comfort of habit" stage; you do not know that you do know. You draw instinctively on your expertise and systems to serve the high-level needs of the client.

Table 1.4   The Master Practitioner

The Level 4 Consultant: The Master Practitioner	
Step 4	*Spiritual*
Consultant growth stage	The Master Practitioner
Buyer type	The economic buyer
Market positioning	Strategic partnership
Needs analysis	Strategic wants
Learning stage	Unconscious competent
Human dimension	Soul/spiritual

Leaving a Legacy

The mastery stage is the ultimate goal for the Odyssey consultant. It can take five to seven years or more of dedicated, consistent application and perseverance. That's at least 10,000 hours focused on doing the right things and not simply drifting along, taking each working day as it comes. You are constantly seeking out new challenges and opportunities for growth and evolving in mind-set and skill set with each one.

The irony is that you perform at this level with a sense of ease. You are not selling your products; you are not forcing your point of view. You work in partnership with the top minds in client companies to find the best ways of adding value and achieving strategic objectives. You have a direct connection with the ultimate economic buyer. Trust and mutual respect is not in question. You become the confidante for business leaders and are the sounding board for high net worth individuals and management teams.

You are in the zone and draw on your extensive experience and learning to create significant strategic value for your client/partner.

Peer respect has been earned at Level 4. You tend to think in terms of legacy. In Imelda's case, she focuses on a combination of activities: Writing, partnering with a select group of Ideal Clients, and working with other consultants, mentoring them as they move from Levels 1 and 2 to Level 3 and beyond. The rewards are less to do with financial gain and are more about making a significant contribution to the world of business in conjunction with fulfilling her personal purpose.

Level 4 is about partnership with the client organization. There's honesty, openness, vulnerability, total respect, and confidence. There are no real questions about why you are there. You are embedded, you work closely with the client, and your valued contribution is recognized.

Odyssey in Action I

Whit Mitchell, Working In Sync, Hanover, New Hampshire

The Trusted Advisor Breakthrough

Whit Mitchell says that he took a backwards route into consulting. He was an accomplished rower in high school, and when he went on to the University of New Hampshire, a chance opportunity lead him into coaching the sport.

He says: "That's when I discovered a passion for getting people from point A to point B a bit quicker than they had been going." When he left college, he started his own business, bringing together his exercise physiology major with his passion for coaching athletes, to create outdoor experiential training programs for a wide range of clients.

He was, at that time, the quintessential Good Soldier. Enthusiastic, professional committed to doing the best job he possibly could. But inexperienced. He had commoditized his expertise and was selling solutions to a client base that could quite possibly have gone elsewhere for the same service.

When he discovered experiential learning, he diversified into executive coaching and quickly collected several high profile clients, including United Airlines and Mobil Oil. He ran corporate executive retreats, where he would lead groups of execs on outdoor programs designed to teach them about leadership and team dynamics. Whit's Competent Warrior years were good … but they were not great.

"I found that most of the work that I was getting was a one- or two-day team building event. Or I'd do an open-invitation seminar, where anyone could come along. I was making enough to pay the bills, but it was all very short term. There wasn't a whole lot of what I'd call stickability to it."

Whit had the sense that he was missing out on something, that there was work out there that was more valuable, more worthwhile, more fulfilling. So he went looking for pathways out of what he was doing, and discovered Odyssey.

He signed up with the Odyssey Business of Consulting program and spent five days in Dublin, Ireland working through the coursework with eight other participants. "Most of my contracts were between $3,500 and $7,000 for a one- or two-day program and a little bit of follow up. Within three months of going with Odyssey, I secured a year-long deal worth $200,000."

The transformation was dramatic. The one and two day programs fell away. He stopped providing product-based solutions and began developing lasting, long term relationships with great clients, clients who came back to him again and again, and became his best referrers. Instead of talking to function heads and HR people, he established direct connections with VPs and CEOs. Whit changed the way he thought about his business, his clients, and even himself.

In securing that first $200K contract, he was, he admits, shocked at his own audacity. "I walked into the CEO's office of a small manufacturing company in New Hampshire, gave him the price and he said: 'Great! When do we get started?' I was flabbergasted. I walked out and got in my car and yelled at the top of my lungs, I couldn't believe it."

It would be wrong however to think that Whit was simply chancing his arm. He was a consulting professional with two decades of experience dealing with a range of corporate buyers. He had worked on executive programs at Columbia and Harvard. A who's who of top 100 companies had been through his hands.

The difference however is that he had managed to transform his experience and expertise into a high value proposition for the client and that had similarly transformed his earning potential. Whit puts it like this: "If they hire me for a year, and the value is five to ten times greater than what they're paying me, well, they're not bad mathematicians."

But to really engage the power of that experience, Whit had to change the way he thought about his clients. "Odyssey," says Whit, "helped me understand how to approach people as peers rather than being scared of them."

Overcoming that fear has been central to Whit's success since then. "Once I had the confidence to go and seek that kind of work and develop peer relationships with CEOs, things have been very different. For example, I've developed a great relationship with a bank CEO and that client has given me four years of great work."

"I deal very little now with the people who need permission to spend money, I just go right to the top. Today, I'm meeting with the CEO of a small company and I feel perfectly comfortable walking in there and chatting with her about what's going on. Odyssey gave me the boot in the pants to go have these conversations."

Odyssey in Action II

Dr. Shayne Tracy, CEO, Executive Strong, Ontario, Canada

The Veterinarian That Never Was

I was at an executive round table, facilitating a basic personal assessment exercise. It was real Good Soldier stuff; transactional, generic, product based designed to answer questions like: What's my style? What are my strengths? What are my liabilities? One of the people taking part was the vice-president of a retail company, a long-established family business, nearly seventy years old, with twenty odd stores around the country. They sold safety boots, overalls, work clothes, and that sort of thing.

After we had finished the exercise, he asked me to come in and do something similar with his executive team. As it would turn out, "team" probably wasn't the best way of describing the group. It was made up of the members of two families, and as is frequently the case with family businesses, there was a lot of baggage at and under the table. All kinds of conflicts, petty and otherwise, divided them.

I came in and began the work, but as I progressed, it became clear that the problems the company had were not going to be solved by a basic assessment exercise. A couple of years earlier, I might not have been alive to that. I had been a Good Soldier, I was selling product, getting revenues in and couldn't really see beyond the next training course or workshop.

But now I saw clearly that the client's needs exceeded my program, so I used that basic transactional intervention to leverage the conversation and begin a sort of preliminary strategic planning exercise: Where are we now? Where do we want to go? How are we going to get there? I was moving things forward to Level 2; I was still basically offering a product, I wasn't embedded, but my portfolio of solutions offered considerably more value than an assessment module possibly could.

I now had a much better perspective on the client's needs. What's more, that original Level 1 exercise had given me enough exposure to the client that he trusted me sufficiently to take it to next level. I was introduced to the president, the son of the founder.

And now the real story began to emerge. The original founder, this man's father, had died two years previously and the son had taken over the business, which was now losing market share, and rapidly. The larger box stores, the Walmarts and so on, were starting to come in and eat his lunch, and the executive team really hadn't done much about it. They were getting great compensation and their heads were in the sand. There was no innovation, no change.

The other thing that emerged was that the deceased founder had a very authoritarian management style. This had left a legacy of bad feeling and damaged relationships, and the son felt he had to adopt a more collaborative style to help redeem the situation. It wasn't working, not least because there was very little talent in the executive group. They were operating a very old business model, but were still able to live quite nicely off the avails, and that bred complacency.

Outside business experience was almost entirely absent. The siblings worked in the business during the summer, and were then automatically enrolled in the company when they graduated, frequently with nothing better than a college diploma. On top of that, there had been no management development or training. From where I stood, all I could see was a highly insular management group with very few management skills.

And while everyone gave the appearance of getting on well, underneath that façade was an undercurrent of seething animosity. "He doesn't do this right, I don't like how he did that, his judgment is flawed …" Meanwhile, the company was losing a lot of money.

I wrote a report—the REC, or Recommendation—as a result of that planning session, and that report then gave me an opportunity to sit down with the president and go over what was being said by the various team members. It was during this meeting that the turning point came.

The president turned to me and said, "You know Shayne, my father thought he was giving me a gift by passing this company along to me but in fact he's given me a millstone around my neck. I never really wanted to be a president of a company. I wanted to be a veterinarian."

It was a very powerful statement, and one that could only have been delivered in an atmosphere of trust. If I had merely been the guy who facilitated the executive assessments, I would not have heard that statement. If I had carried out the planning exercise and walked away, I would not have heard that statement. Through my in-depth engagement with the company, I had become this man's Trusted Advisor. I was inside the tent. I was at the point where I could say to him, "Well, what kind of help do you need?"

He shrugged his shoulders. "I really don't know."

So I proposed a full Business Management Review (BMR), which would include succession planning to smooth his transition out of the company. The issues that this process turned up were many and various. Long story short, we ended up assessing over 200 employees, initiating cultural diagnostics, restructuring the management team and departments, and orchestrating exit packages for a number of employees. We also brought in a range of subcontractors to re-engineer almost every aspect of the company's business; sales, marketing logistics, technology, retail, finances …

When we began our Organizational Development Intervention (ODI) with the company, sales stood at $19 million. When we left a year and a half later, they were $28 million. We went from doing a one day assessment, plus a report for $2,500, to billing just over a quarter of a million dollars.

Ultimately, the company was sold, and its president, while he never real-ized his ambition to become a vet, retired and now volunteers regularly at an animal shelter.

Chapter Summary

The four parallel process levels illustrate how successful consultants progress through their careers. At Level 1, the Good Soldier enters the profession and begins by selling product-based solutions such as assessments and training to the client organization.

Once they have built sufficient experience and a strong reputation, they expand their range of solutions and reach the second step on their Odyssey journey: Level 2, the Competent Warrior. Level 3 is the Trusted Advisor stage, attained by few within the industry, where the consultant becomes a change agent and works with the problem owner to customize business solutions for the client's particular needs.

Level 4, Master Practitioner, is achieved only by elite consultants. This is the level at which the expert business advisor and the client partner in peer-level respect, developing innovative solutions designed to address the long-term visions and objectives for the client and industry.

Calls to Action

We recommend you take time out to review your mind-set and positioning regarding the four levels of consulting. Use the following calls to action to trigger changes in your thinking:

1. Review the four levels as set out in this chapter. Which level(s) are you at right now in your Odyssey business of consulting?

   _____

   _____

   _____

2. In any one assignment and at any one time, a consultant may occupy different levels in the model. In the following table (Table 1.5), list six key client tasks that you are engaged in right now. State which level you are operating at in each case and then itemize the implications of each of those tasks.

Table 1.5   Call to Action 2—List Six Key Tasks

	Task	*Level*	*Why (Implications)*
1			
2			
3			
4			
5			
6			

3. Taking each of the tasks specified in question two, assess each one to see how it might be transformed into a higher level intervention.

———————————————————————————————
———————————————————————————————
———————————————————————————————
———————————————————————————————
———————————————————————————————

4. Where do you see yourself operating in five years' time? Which of the four levels can you reasonably expect to achieve?

———————————————————————————————
———————————————————————————————
———————————————————————————————
———————————————————————————————
———————————————————————————————

Appendix I

In essence, Odyssey is about learning the language, the modus operandi, and the strategic intentions of the Level 3 and Level 4 consultants and understanding how these differ from those of the Level 1 and Level 2 consultants (Figure 1.4).

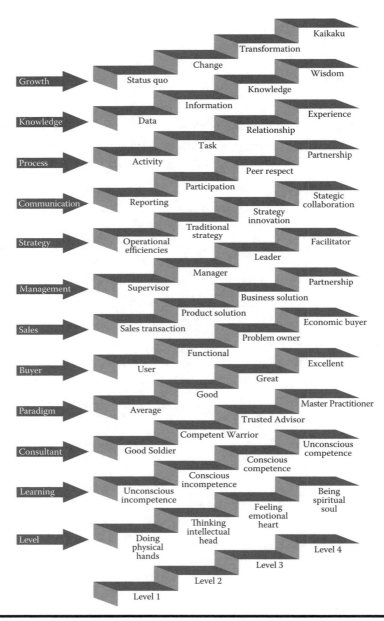

Figure 1.4   Systems thinking—the four parallel process levels.

Bibliography

Bellman, G. M. (1990). *The Consultant's Calling*. San Francisco: Jossey-Bass Inc.

Block, P. (2011). *Flawless Consulting: A Guide to Getting Your Expertise Used* (3rd ed.). San Francisco: Jossey-Bass Inc.

Bonnstetter, B. J. (2010). *If I Knew Then, What I Know Now*. Scottsdale, AZ: Target Training International Ltd.

Bonnstetter, B. J., Suiter, J. I., & Widrick, R. J. (2012). *The Universal Language DISC*. Scottsdale, AZ: Target Training International Ltd.

Burch, N. (1970). *Four Stages for Learning Any New Skill*. Solana Beach, CA: Gordon Training International.

Demarest, P., & Schoof, H. J. (2011). *Answering the Central Question*. Philadelphia, PA: Heartland Publishing LLC.

Goldsmith, M., & Reiter, M. (2007). *What Got You Here, Won't Get You There*. New York: Hyperion Books, HarperCollins.

Goldsmith, M., & Reiter, M. (2010). *MOJO: How to Get It, How to Keep It, How to Get It Back If You Lose It*. New York: Hyperion Books, HarperCollins.

Johnson, A. (2014). *Pushing Back Entropy*. McDonough, GA: Restoration Publishing.

Marston, W. M., & Bonnstetter, B. J. (2012). *Emotions of Normal People*. Scottsdale, AZ: Target Training International Ltd.

Mitchell, W. (2013). *Working InSync*. Eagle, ID: Aloha Publishing.

Rasiel, E. M. (1999). *The McKinsey Way*. Columbus, OH: McGraw-Hill Books.

Tracy, B. (1993). *Maximum Achievement*. New York: Simon & Schuster.

Tuckman, B. (1965). Developmental sequence in small groups. *Psychological Bulletin, 63*(6), 384–99.

Chapter 2

The Odyssey Arrow Value Engagement Process: Bringing Clarity to Client Needs

- How will you source and engage your Ideal Clients?
- Do you have a business process and system for delivering superb client value and masterful results?

We now come to one of the most important concepts in the consultant's Odyssey. The Odyssey Arrow is a visual representation of the path to the ultimate Odyssey goal, which is to engage with your Ideal Clients on key assignments to deliver superb value and produce masterful results. The Odyssey Arrow is the business development system of the Odyssey process and provides practical, step-by-step guidelines showing how consultants move from identifying their Ideal Clients all the way through to delivering a Level 3 or Level 4 intervention.

The process that underlies the system is dynamic and versatile and has been adapted by high caliber consultants with many years of consulting and business experience. Trusting and following the process is an imperative. Practitioners of the Odyssey Arrow have learned two valuable points when engaging with the process (Figure 2.1):

- Give it due time and respect.
- Never go to the next step until you are satisfied that the step you are on is complete to both your and the client's satisfaction.

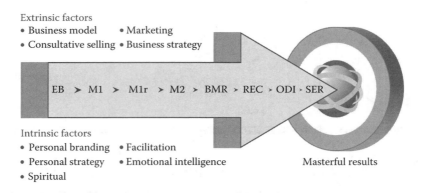

Extrinsic factors
• Business model   • Marketing
• Consultative selling • Business strategy

EB ➤ M1 ➤ M1r ➤ M2 ➤ BMR ➤ REC ➤ ODI ➤ SER

Intrinsic factors
• Personal branding • Facilitation
• Personal strategy • Emotional intelligence
• Spiritual   Masterful results

Figure 2.1   The Odyssey Arrow.

Extrinsic and Intrinsic Factors

Before embarking on the process described by the Odyssey Arrow, you will need to lock down a series of extrinsic and intrinsic factors itemized in the previously mentioned graphic. These factors comprise the key business and personal metrics of your consulting business.

Every consultant must set out the financial, marketing, consultative selling, and business strategies of their consulting business before they can credibly discuss these aspects with a client in respect of the client's business. These issues will be discussed in more detail in Chapter 5 (The Business behind Consulting).

The intrinsic factors, outlined further in Chapter 6 (The Mental Game), must also be carefully considered. An awareness of your own personal branding, your personal strategy, your facilitation style, your emotional intelligence, and your spiritual connectivity all contribute to the connectivity of who you are and what you do in consulting.

Once the extrinsic factors have been processed and systemized, and the intrinsic self-awareness journey is under way, the Odyssey business system, as captured by the Odyssey Arrow, can be fully and successfully deployed.

The Arrow Legend Explained

The Value Engagement Practices

Executive Briefing (EB)—establishing initial contact with the Ideal Client base

Meeting One (M1)—first meeting with client

Meeting One Response Letter (M1r)—as described

Meeting Two (M2)—the second meeting, together with any additional interactions

Business Management Review (BMR)—key strategic information gathering exercise

The Value Integration Practices

Recommendation (REC)—based on a portfolio of solutions

Organizational Development Intervention (ODI)

Summary Evaluation Report (SER)

We will review the first five value engagement practices in detail in this chapter and the three value integration or implementation practices in the following chapter. Before we look at the EB, however, we will consider the Ideal Client.

The Ideal Client Profile: Who, What, When, Where, Why, How

The Odyssey Arrow describes how you work at building value for your business, but before that process, you have to prepare the groundwork for identifying and cultivating your Ideal Clients. Consider the following Ideal Client profile and imagine how the following operative questions might be applied to your consulting business.

Who Is My Ideal Client Number 1 Category (IC1)?

An IC1 can be an individual and/or an organization. Here is an example of an Ideal Client categorization:

IC1: My Ideal Client is John Jones, a 42-year-old CEO owner of ABC Company with personal worth of $10 million minimum and realizable business assets of $100 million. He is a like-minded person, and we have an immediate peer-level respect for one another. He is courageous and action orientated, helpful, and collaborative. Above all, he is open to change, learning, and growth.

What Is My Ideal Client Looking for?

He wishes to capitalize on his gain potential and to reduce his potential for losses. In addition, he wants to leverage market opportunities, innovation, new product development, cultural change management, strategic initiatives, and more. He is often unclear or inarticulate, but he knows what is required when it is revealed to him. He is looking for a strategic solution.

When Is My Ideal Client in the Market?

There are a range of triggers here. An "if not now, when?" moment can arise as a result of an external shock. Frequently, there is frustration in relation to the slow pace of change or growth relative to the potential. For the entrepreneurial mind, the moment is always now.

Where Do My Ideal Clients Find Me?

The EB is a key point of contact for new clients. In addition, professional introductions and referrals from other Ideal Clients represent a pipeline for new business.

Why Will My Ideal Clients Engage Me?

The reason is, first, because of a meeting of minds and philosophies. There is an acceptance that they themselves cannot do what needs to be done because they are part of the problem or challenge. In other words, they are too close to the situation to maintain an objective perspective on the big picture. There is a sense of relief that they can partner and collaborate with a credible expert.

How Will We Work Together?

By building trust in a series of incremental stages, showing the way to the achievement of clearly defined objectives, as defined by the Odyssey Arrow (Figure 2.2).

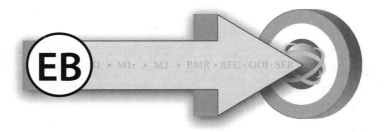

Figure 2.2 Executive Briefing.

Executive Briefing

One powerful way to attract your Ideal Clients is to present an EB or a series of EBs on subjects tailored to engage their interest. You can achieve credibility and respect and build trust by demonstrating your depth of knowledge on a subject or subjects and your understanding of the prospective client's business challenges. Your prospective clients do not want to be sold to; they want to be educated and offered solutions to the challenges they are experiencing. You are a thought leader.

The EB will generate initial appointments, provide an opportunity for client buy-in for your services, and stimulate the prospective client to take action in the moment.

In our experience, there is a range of client challenges that can draw clients to EBs and stimulate consulting opportunities:

- The company is in growth mode and needs help.
- Executives overly focused on day-to-day operational issues and lack strategic direction.
- The leader is focused on working "in the business" as opposed to working strategically "on the business."
- The company sees the need to invest in talent management and succession planning.
- The company has a new president/CEO/executive team who wants to change the culture and potential of the organization.
- The company is experiencing competitive pressures.
- The company is losing or is in fear of losing talent and/or business market share.

These briefings are generally low cost or no cost seminars/workshops presented to an invited audience, where you showcase your business and whet the client's appetite for the services you provide. Your aim is to favorably alter a prospective client's decision criteria or biases by using data, information, pain points, a touch of drama, and a call to action.

To grow and maintain a healthy client pipeline, consultants are advised to consider at least four EBs annually.

Our Story

An alternative EB option is to partner with other professional organizations. I recently collaborated with our accountant on a series of four EBs run on the last Monday of each month. We presented relevant topics, including "How to Put the Mojo Back into Your Business" and "How to Reinvent your Entrepreneurial Spirit." We also brought in specialists to present particular topics and a celebrity speaker to add further traction to the briefings.

Partnering with your local chamber is another worthwhile option, or handpicking your audience, either from your client base or from the market sector in which you specialize. You could offer an in-house EB at corporate level, bringing the senior executives together for an 8 a.m. business breakfast. To maximize effectiveness, always pick topics that are both relevant and timely.

The EB is a critical first step, designed to introduce you to potential clients and to prompt them to critically assess their own businesses. The EB will help the participants recognize challenges or opportunities in their business, which they would like to address. This realization will trigger the M1, which is your first one-on-one meeting with the prospective client.

Meeting One

The first meeting provides you with the platform to explore the possibility of further engagement between you and your prospective client. Outlined here is the precise format recommended in the Odyssey Arrow system (Figure 2.3).

After the standard introductions and rapport-building niceties, there comes a "signal point," when you set the course of the process and how it is to be conducted by saying something like the following:

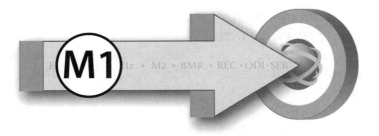

Figure 2.3   Meeting One.

"My objective (purpose) today is to gain an understanding of you and your organization (or this assignment/project), and to give you an insight into who we are and what we do ... Is that OK?"

Agreement, even a nodding agreement, puts an unwritten contract in place, which allows you to ask questions and explore possibilities. As you work through the process, consider both your own and your client's position within the four parallel process levels. As an accurate picture of their situation emerges, ask yourself, are they your Ideal Client?

The M1 questions are set out here in three stages, designed to bring you deeper into the client's organization, project, or assignment. Frequently, consultants will ask the step one questions but lack the confidence or expertise to continue through to the metrics and clarifying objectives questions. Used correctly, the M1 questions represent powerful tools for analyzing the prospective client's mind-set and the issues they face.

Do not, however, become a victim of the questions. It is important not to stick slavishly to the list set out here but to respond to the client as the issues emerge. In essence, you are taking the client through each of the four levels discussed in Chapter 1:

- The hand: How are things working on a day-to-day basis?
- The head: What is the thinking behind these processes?
- The heart: How do you feel about it?
- The soul: What is the ideal situation?

The consultant should always go into the meeting with this attitude: "While I would like more business, I do not need it." This phrase helps to set the tone of the meeting and keeps the focus on the client, not the consultant. It is recommended, for business growth purposes, that the consultant set up at least four M1s per month to keep the client funnel flowing.

The M1 Questions—Step 1: Situation Analysis—Past, Present, Future

- Tell me about you and/or your company, its history, and its development.
- What is going well?
- What are the current challenges?
- Where does it hurt? What is your biggest unsolved problem?
- How long have things been this way? Why?

- What is your current goal?
- What are you really trying to achieve in your business?
- What is your business philosophy?
- What is the biggest obstacle to achieving your goal?
- What are you doing about that obstacle?
- Where will you be in three years' time?

- If you were to take a performance improvement initiative, what would make it worthwhile?
- What are the critical metrics that you use to check the pulse of your business? List the top five or six.
- What has been your experience with improvement initiatives and earlier consulting interventions?
- What do you believe is the best way to approach change?
- What opportunities are open to you?
- What priority do you give each of these opportunities?

- How committed are you to your own personal and professional development?
- How do you create business advantage?
- How would you describe the culture in your organization?
- How would you characterize morale?
- How would your customers describe you?
- What is your business model?
- How does it serve you and your business now?
- Will it still serve you in three to five years' time?

- Is there anything further you would like to add?
- What questions would you ask if you were me?
- Knowing what you now know about XYZ, would you have acted as you did?

The M1 Questions—Step 2: Clarifying Assignment Objectives

- What three macro outcomes, in order of importance, do you want from this assignment?
- Waving a magic wand across the problem, what would an ideal scenario/outcome look like?
- On an operational level, what difference would this outcome make to employees and others?
- How would it impact your customers?
- How would your board of directors recognize the change?
- What is your biggest concern about undertaking this assignment now?
- What do you need to know about me?
- What bottom-line metrics can be measured to prove this assignment is a success?
- What else do we need to talk about to make this meeting worthwhile?

The M1 Questions—Step 3: Establishing the Measures (Metrics) of Success and Value

- Can you quantify the impact of this problem, opportunity, or change in dollar/euro terms?
- What are the implications for you if this assignment fails?
- What direct effect will this project have on performance, productivity, sales, profit?
- How will this assignment affect cultural factors such as morale?
- How will we know you are happy?

Add Questions Appropriately to Dig Deeper

- How do you mean?
- Tell me more?
- Would you still hire person X? Would you still …?

Having completed a thorough note taking and fact-finding M1, you will then "pen sell"; thank them for their overview, which gave you an excellent appreciation of the client's business.

You then outline your business model for your potential client, using stories and connecting your business model to the potential solutions for their challenges and opportunities. If you cannot help the client or if their challenges are outside your area of expertise, be upfront about it.

I recently met with a potential client, and as I listened to their situation, it emerged that they required IT expertise. I simply recommended that they solve those issues as a priority and perhaps revert to me once they had resolved those issues. The secret is do not try to be all things to all people. If IT, finance, social media, or other identified issues are not your area of specialization or expertise, make recommendations that they seek appropriate advice.

If, on the other hand, the challenges, objectives, and issues raised are within your portfolio of expertise and remit, let the potential client know that you will review the meeting and write a response letter reviewing the key points of the discussion, giving a more in-depth overview of your business and making a recommendation to move forward.

The Discovery Audit

Comprehensive diagnosis is essential to deliver an effective result-based REC and value-based ODI—both of which are discussed in detail in the next chapter. Right from the first meeting—the M1—you are examining the scope and nature of the consulting assignment before you. You are consistently uncovering the client's opportunities, threats, weaknesses, and strengths. You are "getting your arms around" the consulting assignment and working to bring more clarity to the organizational challenges the client is struggling with. Very often a discovery audit is conducted as an independent, fee-based activity project before the REC stage.

Diagnostic Methods

There are several methods of gathering facts and information about the client organization. These include:

- Records
- Special occasions/events
- Observations
- Interviews

- Questionnaires
- Orientation briefings
- Climate surveys
- Assessments
- Focus groups
- Organization surveys

Growth curve analysis, job benchmarking, competency, behavior and values measurement, and financial analytics all have a role in the consultant's diagnostic toolkit and may be deployed at different stages of the Odyssey Arrow process.

In our book, *Successful Entrepreneurial Management: How to Create Personal and Business Advantage*, we discuss the six-link chain of resources, which govern the performance of the organization. These resources are money, product, physical, intangible, time, and people. Using the six-resource chain as a template to model the client's business gives the consultant a powerful diagnostic tool (Figure 2.4).

- Money: Is there a lack of working capital? Is there overborrowing? Is the working capital not working due to poor cash flow management, unrealistic costing, collections, and overgenerous budgeting/spending?
- Product: What is the product offering and how does it measure up? Is the client delivering outstanding customer service? Is service delivery as good as it could be? Are packaging and design needs being met?
- Physical: Assessing the strengths and weaknesses of the client's location, equipment, and technology. Are they fit for purpose?

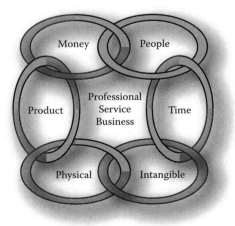

Figure 2.4   The six resource model.

■ Intangibles: What about staff morale, levels of motivation, engagement, respect, culture, ethos, corporate philosophy, and image? Are low standards in this area poisoning company performance? How do you measure the goodwill of the company?

■ Time: How are key resources deploying their time? Is there wastage? How could time be better allocated by key resources within the organization?

■ People: Where are the emotional, psychological, and cultural choke points? Is there a lack of leadership, management, or specific talent? Are personal issues within teams hindering progress? Is there an openness to change? Are there performance issues?

Road blocks and choke points can exist at any one of these links. People working in organizations often fail to identify the weakest link, for a variety of reasons. The fact is that the weakest link affects and controls the overall success of the six resources. If you invest resources in a link which is not the weakest link, you do not improve overall results. In fact, strengthening a link which is not the weakest can often weaken the entire chain of resources. The consultant's role is that of an objective observer and advisor, providing clarity, focus, and capacity to align an organization's resource chain.

The Problems Associated with Discovery

To restate: Discovery is about answering questions to bring clarity, focus, and capacity to the assignment. Be mindful of the pitfalls in this process. Here are several common errors consultants make when seeking to diagnose problems in a client organization:

■ Mistaking effects for causes—going for the quick solution without conducting proper diagnostics.

■ Failure to widely canvass all stakeholders, e.g., board of directors, customers, and lower ranks.

■ The functional eye—jumping to a quick functional solution rather than exploring all possible causes and long-term implications.

■ Listening to the best view only—making decisions based on limited information without conducting full, due process investigations.

■ "It's urgent and must be sorted out tomorrow"—firefighting and reacting rather than resolving issues at source and eliminating causes.

■ Getting sidetracked—not keeping the client focused on key result areas and majoring on minor issues and "white herrings."

The Benefits of Good Discovery

The overall objective of the discovery phase is to collate all of the necessary material to arrive at a more accurate, targeted REC. One of the benefits of an excellent diagnostic process is that it cements the level of collaboration between consultant and client from an early stage in the assignment. Effectively, it provides you with a license to go ahead with the course of action already planned or about to be outlined in the REC stage.

Meeting One Response Letter

The purpose of the M1r is threefold: to capture the essence of your discussion at the M1, to give the client a deeper insight into the style and approach of your consulting business, and to make a recommendation on how the assignment/project can move forward (Figure 2.5).

At the M1, the client does 90% of the talking. The M1r letter is the opportunity to demonstrate that you have captured everything that was said, both explicitly and implicitly, that is, reading between the lines. In conveying that information, it is important that you do not theorize what the client said, but use "native" language—in other words, the client's own phraseology— to describe their situation. In the following sample letter, the phrases in inverted commas are phrases that the client has used and are lifted directly from the M1.

Writing a good, professional response letter is what separates the amateur from the professional. The novice consultant will grasp at the client and rush out a proposal. The reality is that you have to slow down to go faster. By progressing gradually through the stages of the Odyssey Arrow, you establish credibility, peer-level respect, and professionalism. You are conveying to the client that you understand their situation and objectives and where it

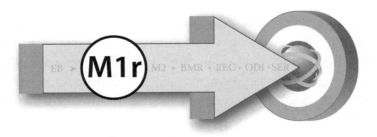

Figure 2.5   Meeting One Response Letter.

hurts for them and their business. They are developing trust and the expectation that you can help them fulfil their purpose and vision and reawaken their passion for their business.

In addition to reviewing all that was discussed at the M1, the M1r also gives you an opportunity to tell the client a little more about your consulting practice and to sketch out the action steps that should follow.

Sample M1r Letter

Dear Andrew,

Thank you for the overview and insight you gave me into your practice during your visit to our office on Thursday, 23rd March.

The purpose of my letter is threefold:

1. To capture the essence of our discussion
2. To give you a deeper insight into the style and approach of Century Management
3. To make a recommendation on how we move forward from here

1. *ACP Engineering—An Overview of Our Discussion*

You gave me an excellent outline of the background, history, and developmental structure of your practice since it was founded in 1983. You explained how the business grew from its origins and opened a second office in Dublin.

You described the partnership and management structure within ACP Engineering in some detail. Last year, you started to ask the question "Where are we going?" and made some decisions around client focus and the kind of business that you sought. You described the biggest problem right now as "how to market, sell, and set strategy" for the business.

It is often difficult to "control the discussion" in partnership meetings and talk meaningfully about a future target. In fact, your functional expertise—"being good engineers"—may be overshadowing your business acumen. You see your own job in the near future as "pointing the way forward" and developing a map for the future growth of the practice.

Your own immediate vision for ACP Engineering is to develop a high-quality, well-respected practice, which is three to four times its current size. Getting collective buy-in and overcoming any scepticism or resistance to the missionary nature of this focus may be one of the immediate challenges to overcome.

You described the culture in the office as "good quality without fuss" and the culture in the second office as "more professional." A good spirit pervades the organiazation and you have regular social nights throughout the year.

Your revenue last year was €15 million, with a profit margin of 20%. There are four shareholders in the business. You envisage strong growth over the next five years and would like to buy out the retiring shareholder in two years' time. As a professional services firm, your staff represent the highest cost item at €X million, which is consistent with industry norms. You said that you would like to increase shareholder value and return on investment.

Personally, your private ambition is to prepare the business for acquisition, merger, or takeover in about five years. You would like to be in a position to explore your interests in art and design, about which you spoke passionately.

I hope I have grasped the essence of your input to the discussion. Our meeting was free-flowing and informal, so I may not have captured all the ideas, facts, and emotions that were expressed. If I have missed a point, I would greatly appreciate your feedback.

2. *The Century Management Approach*

Century Management has developed an excellent reputation for our consultative approach to business development. We are primarily a strategy consultancy, engaged in strategic human performance improvement, culminating in organization-wide systemic and cultural change, augmented by tailored learning and development programs.

We believe that maximizing human performance and business development should be a continuous, long-term process rather than a series of quick-fix, short-term, do-something-for-the-sake-of-it type events.

I attach a copy of our business model, which I explained in our meeting, together with our corporate document titled *Future Focus*. This will give you an outline of the Century Management philosophy, approach, and solutions for individual, team, and organization development. Also included is a commentary from ten of our clients, which details the interventions they are currently applying within their organizations with our support.

3. *To Progress from Here*

From our initial meeting, I believe your needs and objectives are wholly within the portfolio of solutions that Century Management provide. To move your practice from where you are now to where you want to go may mean addressing issues, including change management, cultural transformation, and strategic direction, as well as moving from a management focus to a leadership driven style.

Right now, I need a more in-depth perspective of the heartbeat of your practice, and until then, I would resist making specific recommendations about how to deal with the challenges you outlined at our meeting.

To progress matters, I would like to set up a BMR. I suggest we meet around 3 p.m. and work into the evening and over dinner, then follow up with a three-hour session the next morning. We will take you through a BMR process during this exercise.

Before the BMR, I would like to meet with each of the management teams directly on a one-to-one basis. This is the single best way for me to get close to your business and put me in a position to make recommendations that can help you achieve your objectives.

The primary aim of the BMR is to explore, assess, and complete an analysis of the current situation and thinking within the senior team. More importantly, it sets the scene for us to scope out a fuller organizational solution (if necessary) in an informed way. Collective buy-in is always an essential part of any successful intervention.

Please discuss this in broad terms with your partners in preparation for our review discussion on Monday next (date and time). I will then outline the format, fee structure, and all the other details.

I look forward to meeting you on Monday.

Yours sincerely,
Imelda K. Butler
Managing Director

Meeting Two

As suggested in the sample letter, it is always a good idea to communicate with the client after the M1r letter has been sent and clarify that you have captured their situation as accurately as possible and to make sure that

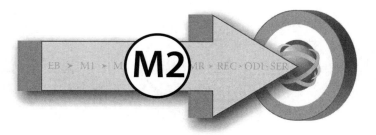

Figure 2.6   Meeting Two.

nothing has been omitted. A follow-up meeting—the M2—is recommended to provide these clarifications (Figure 2.6).

The M2, and M3, M4, and even M5, if required, have another vital function. The M1 was all about understanding the picture in the client's mind: the obstacles faced, the project or assignment under consideration, and so on. The reality of course is that it is rare that there is only one person involved. The M2 and subsequent meetings are designed to provide a forum for other key players to give their perspective on the issues under discussion.

A series of one-to-one meetings may be required to provide input from senior management, partners, function heads, and so on, to give the consultant a full 360-degree view of the organization. Finding out where everyone is coming from is also an essential part of achieving full buy-in for any interventions that may be recommended down the line.

Business Management Review

The BMR is one of the most powerful tools in a consultant's kit. It provides an excellent, low-risk way for both client and consultant to gain a thorough understanding of the business (Figure 2.7).

The purpose of the BMR is:

- To listen attentively … The client team to themselves, but more importantly, you to the client
- To facilitate an honest open session … Question gently, reflectively comment
- To observe how they rationalize their world … The picture in their mind
- To establish individual and collective mind-sets … Ask, "What is emerging for all of you?"
- To assess the possibility of an ODI of whatever nature

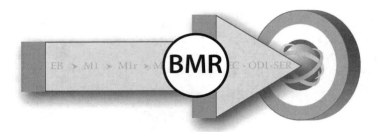

Figure 2.7 Business Management Review.

- To determine levels of peer-level respect and capabilities
- To understand the culture and nuances in the organization

This process not only gives you the information you need to move forward with the client, it maintains the participatory dynamic begun with the M2, which will be vital both in achieving a deep, clear understanding of the business and in maintaining stakeholder buy-in.

The BMR is also central to the process of building relationships within the client organization. As we saw in Chapter 1, establishing peer-level respect is a core prerequisite to Level 3 Trusted Advisor and Level 4 Master Practitioner interventions. The BMR provides an excellent vehicle for fostering that mutual respect and paving the way for delivering masterful results.

To better illustrate how a BMR is set up, here is an e-mail sent to participants in the ACP Engineering BMR in the aftermath of the M2 and subsequent one-to-one meetings.

Sample BMR Setup E-mail

Greetings from Imelda K. Butler

Thank you for your openness and honesty in our one-to-one conversations in preparation for our BMR on 18th–19th of May in the Heritage Hotel (which will start at 3 p.m. on the 18th and finish at 11 a.m. on the 19th of May).

The primary objective of the "Heritage" meeting is to allow each person to articulate their view of the business to ascertain individual perspectives and help establish the collective mind-set. Listening to you explain the various scenarios and strategies will be my primary objective.

To help make the occasion as valuable as possible, can I ask you to prepare a presentation on a flip-chart page or two, following this format:

Step 1: Current Situation Analysis

How would you describe the current status of the business? What is working well? What is not working so well? What needs changing? What are you good at and not good at? What is "the great unsaid?" What do you most value—as an individual—about working in your company? What is the baseline?

Step 2: The History

What have been the significant points in your development path that have led you to here? How do you look back on your history? (a short appraisal).

Step 3: The Future

Where do you see the practice in the years ahead? Be specific. What is your vision for the company? What hopes and concerns do you have about the future? What are the macro objectives? Where do you want to be?

Step 4: The How

How will you get from where you are to where you want to be? What are the critical success factors that will need to happen to ensure your vision for the future is accomplished? What could stop/hinder you from achieving your desired outcome?

Here are the presentation guidelines:

■ Each person makes a fifteen- to twenty-minute presentation. (We draw lots for the order.)
■ Flip charts allow us to stick contributions up on a wall for a panoramic display as we progress. This way we can see the full picture, any emerging points, and "the obvious" all at once. (No fancy computer presentations please, that we can do later.)
■ Be bold here … use some color and/or diagrams or creativity to capture your message.
■ Isolate three to four MACRO points in each step rather than getting too MICRO on operational issues.

The Heritage session is primarily about investigation and evidence gathering. In medical terms, it is the examination stage. After this session, Century Management will be well placed to recommend an intervention for ACP

Engineering. After preliminary discussions, we do have several scenarios in mind, but we want to complete a thorough "due process" before outlining any solutions.

If you are at all unclear, please call me. Otherwise, I look forward to meeting you in the Heritage.

Imelda K. Butler

The BMR in Action

There are many different ways in which they may be conducted. By taking the event off-site, you are breaking with the work routine and removing the tunnel effect that can exist in an office environment, where everyone's thinking remains locked into their own particular department. Giving the BMR a social dimension greatly enhances the potential for openness, creativity, and innovation.

The follow-up session the next day allows everyone to review the perspectives and insights that the previous evening's discussion produced. You review the emerging picture overnight, isolate the key issues, and give the participants an opportunity to feedback on all that went before.

This overnight structure is not essential. You can customize the experience to the organization; meet at 9 a.m., and continue through the day if that's more appropriate. It is very important, however, that you retain the Level 3 and Level 4 approach, and that the BMR does not become a workshop or a training type event.

Our Story

At a recent BMR I organized for a client, the overnight structure worked perfectly. By the time their key team had flown in from Europe, it was nearly lunchtime. Presentations were made throughout the afternoon, and then in the evening, there was an opportunity to break down communication barriers and discuss business and strategy in a more informal way. Just as any married couple benefits from breaking out of the everyday environment, an executive team benefits hugely from altered dynamics, from softening the structures that govern how they communicate with each other on a day-to-day basis.

The session the following day gave everyone an opportunity to bring diverse views together and clarify the emerging picture. This phase also gives you, the consultant, an opportunity to present your business model.

Although you do not, at this point, recommend any particular course of action, you provide participants with a view of how you work and an indication of what an intervention might look like.

Sometimes, at a BMR, the consultant will try to do too much. Resist the temptation to transform what is essentially a fact-finding mission into a full-strategy session. Again, slow down to move faster. Do not try to jump the river.

To help illustrate how to follow up a BMR, the following is a sample report emerging from the ACP Engineering BMR.

ACP Engineering—BMR Report

The following report was prepared and presented to the client post the BMR.

ACP Engineering is a fine company, doing most things very well. This should be self-evident to everyone who attended the BMR in the Heritage Hotel on 18th–19th of May. The consistent message coming through from this meeting, as well as each of the six one-to-one sessions that preceded it, was that "the time has come" to move this practice on to a new level to reach its full potential.

There was clear evidence of a simmering sense of frustration with why ACP was not simply "getting on with it." This is a healthy and a necessary catalyst to the step change that is required. The reasons WHY you should transform the practice and HOW you should set such a process in motion will emerge from this "stuckness."

The primary objective of any potential intervention is cultural transformation, change management, and leadership development to better prepare the company to achieve its vision. The latent talent, intellectual prowess, reputation, and sense of camaraderie, all of which were so evident at the BMR, will be vital in helping to "springboard" the practice into the premier league.

The main message emerging from the Heritage meeting is that you are ready, willing, and able. Moreover, you are willing to invest the time and the resources necessary to make change happen as a collective unit. Collectivity and teamwork are vital ingredients of any proposed intervention.

Building the core competencies that are necessary to transform the business is THE critical factor in your long-term success. Dealing with succession planning, talent management, networking, marketing, branding, relationship selling, and internal communications management are all part and parcel of the "education" that is required and the "imagination" that is necessary to move from "the old way of doing things."

The first part of the process will deal with the softer, more psychological factors involved in changing the thinking, attitudes, and business practices of your organization. The more functional and strategic part of the process is about equipping the senior team, in particular, with the mind-set, tools, and techniques to move from being "successful engineers" to being business leaders. In this regard, developing the commercial acumen, leadership robustness, and financial management skills will be critical to your success.

Napoleon said that "men will die for ribbons." When your purpose and reasons are crystal clear—and committed to paper—people become better problem solvers and better communicators. They become more creative, more efficient, and more productive. In a nutshell, when the *why* is strong enough and clear enough, the *how* becomes easier.

The fundamental job of all leaders is to create the vision and then to show the way by putting wheels underneath it. The critical thing is to bring everyone with you. When a whole team moves together, waste is drastically reduced. More importantly, the focus moves from the past and present to the possibilities of the future.

ACP Engineering has a great story to tell. You have to articulate that story to the people who will join your company over the next three to five years, to your Ideal Clients in the market place and to potential business partners and other stakeholders. The time has come to stop telling "the great story" to yourselves alone and start the campaign to convince a whole new audience over the next five years.

Building the underlying confidence of the organization is a key part of this. Building the competencies and skills that are sometimes alien to being a good engineer is equally important. It will take time, dedication, and a new resolve to embed these essential leadership competencies deep into the ethos and culture of ACP Engineering.

The way in which you explain yourself to yourself is called your explanatory style. The following list of verbatim comments from the Heritage meeting gives some clue as to your state of readiness for the organizational process that lies ahead:

- "We are in a period of growth."
- "Jumping to the next level."
- "What is the ACP value proposition?"
- "We are in a state of flux."
- "Busy being engineers."
- "Top ten in Ireland in terms of work."

- "I have learned new things about this team today."
- "We are going to have to change as people."
- "Maybe it is time to eat for the practice."
- "How do we become the best all round practice in the country?"
- "We need something to pull us together."
- "Are we commercially naïve?"
- "Why are we having difficulty attracting senior engineers?"

This is just a flavor to help you appreciate your views of ACP. Next week, I will compile a recommendation to demonstrate how we can move forward together.

Odyssey in Action I

Sergio Motles, Summit Consulting, Santiago, Chile

The Power of the BMR

I always divide the BMR into two sessions, the first in the afternoon and the second the following morning. Holding it at an offsite location is always a good idea because it creates the right kind of atmosphere.

I usually begin at 3 p.m. with a clear agenda. The first session is all about the present and the past. I've asked the participants beforehand to prepare a short presentation, so everybody comes with two flip charts ready-made. In the first session, we're concerned with the first set of charts, which looks at the past and present. The second set, which looks at the future and "the how," we look at in the second session the following day.

They use colors, pictures, or just bullet points, whatever they feel is the best way to transmit their ideas. We hang those on the walls at the beginning of the session that first afternoon. That way, we can see the emerging picture; what the company actually looks like to the people who are running it. It's also a really dynamic process; I try to make it fun. You're moving around; they're moving around. There's an informality about it that helps people to relax and open up about the real issues.

My role is to facilitate and engage everyone in dialogue and to move the process along.

It's vital to nurture an atmosphere of trust. I point out that whatever is being said is being said for the good of the company. You can't have any accusations; it's my job to keep everyone on message and to prevent any kind of hostility from creeping in. I also make sure that whoever's highest in the hierarchy speaks last. That way, anything that's difficult to say has been said before the boss stands up.

At this point, we're not talking about solutions, we're just saying, "This is what's happening with each one of us, this is our experience of our working lives, this is what's not been said up to now …" They talk about what's bugging them and what's stopping them from working as they would like to work.

We break about 7 p.m. or 8 p.m. after I summarize the day. We eat and maybe go to the pool. It's important that everyone stays onsite and that the air of informality and sociability continues all the way through.

The next morning at 8:30 a.m. or 9 a.m., we start again. I outline the agenda for the day. This session is about the future and identifying actions to get there. The previous day, I asked the general manager to speak last. Today, I ask him to speak first. He talks about his vision because everything has to be aligned with his vision. So he goes first, talking about the future as he sees it. Then each member of the team gets up and talks about their view of how things should be. The format is the same as the day before. We use the flipcharts, and each speaker outlines their ideas. As the morning goes by, a vision of the future slowly begins to emerge on the walls.

Once everyone has spoken, I work through the points with them. I say, "Let's summarize, between all of us … What is going to be our main focus, our main objectives over the next year." You end up with no more than eight big issues. Someone will say, "How are we going to do all of this?" I say, "Don't worry about that. Let's deal with the 'what' now, and worry about the 'how' later."

Next, I say, "OK, who's going to take charge here? Who's going to be accountable for each point, for each of the strategic objectives that we've agreed?" And I parcel out each one to the relevant person, together with an agreed time frame within which the objective must be reached. Again, I tell them that we'll talk about how to begin to deal with each objective later. For now, it is enough that there is an internal champion in the company who will take responsibility for striving towards their particular objective.

In my next meeting, I bring in the report from the BMR, and I say, "This is what we agreed, these are the objectives we defined." They might relate to strategic alignment or communication, computer systems or teamwork, whatever. It's at this point I start to unroll the solutions, but as I do, I have already recruited individuals within the company who are accountable for each strategic objective.

I always get a great reaction to these BMRs. By the end of the second day, there's tremendous enthusiasm in the room. People want to talk, but they've never had the opportunity before. By creating the right kind of atmosphere, you can achieve a depth of discovery that you just don't get with any other tool.

I just recently completed a consulting assignment with a Chilean company which specialized in the importation and distribution of playground toys. We went through a very rigorous BMR, which turned up some serious communications issues within the organization. I recommended a four-month program of motivation and coaching, which ultimately transformed the way they did business.

That process was instrumental in creating high levels of trust between us, to the point where I was asked to sit in on management meetings throughout the following year. I helped directly in the finance area, which is my own area of expertise, and coordinated the hiring of other consultants to work on the IT and marketing initiatives.

Within a year, the company had doubled their sales into the Chilean market and had substantially increased exports to other South American companies. Those initial stages of the Odyssey Arrow created huge levels of trust and generated exactly the right environment for me to move from Level 1 to Level 3. I had moved into a position where I was able to provide the client not just with a product but with a truly transformational intervention.

Odyssey in Action II

Dan Grobarchik, Exsell Inc., Green Bay, Wisconsin

It Starts with Finding Ideal Clients

Most consultants know their stuff, but they're terrible sales people. When I saw the Odyssey system, I went "Yes!" This is what I've been teaching for years, and now in addition, you have all of the rest of the Odyssey program to back it up.

A couple of years ago—actually the second time through the Odyssey process—I was introduced to a consulting firm in Milwaukee, Wisconsin. When I started to consult with them, they basically had no clients.

I worked with them to develop the Odyssey value-driven consulting proposition, and within a year, we had six good clients in the mix. Two years in, they've got a bottom line of half a million dollars.

The first thing I had to do was to help them understand who their Ideal Clients are. I was something like two or three years in consulting before I figured this out, though it's very evident in Odyssey. Another thing I've discovered is that you really don't want to take a company that's failing and try to save it; you want good companies so you can help them become great companies.

You're looking for the person that wants to grow their company. They've got to be open. They've got to be willing to change. That's something that really crystallized for me when I went through Odyssey.

How do you know if your prospect meets these criteria? I'm always preaching, "Slow it down, slow it down, take them out to dinner, really get into the guy's head." If you're dealing with people that can actually change, you have a much higher chance of success. You're not looking for a particular skill set; you're looking for a particular attitude. I don't take on any clients or any coaching situations where I don't have a good chance of success.

The next step is to help them with their market prospecting and get their pipeline going. This client had no referrals coming in per se, so we had to begin with the Executive Briefing. I've been doing Executive Briefings for twenty years, so that's an easy one for me to help on.

This company was partnering with a local college in staging its EBs. Typically, when you're doing your own briefing, you can disqualify some people who you know are not and will never be Ideal Clients. That was a little bit of an issue with the college because they had their list and couldn't really say no to anybody. So we had a lot of people coming into the briefings who were just not the right people. They weren't decision makers, and they weren't the owners.

But we worked through that, and we still got two or three good leads out of that first briefing. Two months later, we got two more good leads, and two months after that, two or three more leads. On another occasion, we had a really good HR person at the briefing. She wasn't the decision maker, but she was insightful enough to see value in what we were doing, so she invited us in. We did an in-house briefing and ended up doing some good business with that client.

After a slow start, my client got their Executive Briefings down. They got to know what they were doing, their positioning in the marketplace, and how to present that. Today, the company is just getting to the point where they're starting to get really good referrals, and they will now take over from the Executive Briefing.

We did a lot of rehearsal ahead of the M1. The client started to develop some really good questions and slowed the process way down. We also spent quite a bit of time working on the M1r letter and fine-tuning the process with M2 and M3 meetings.

Next of course is the Business Management Review. Over the last year or two, the principal consultant in this practice has come to define the BMR for himself. He's got it down: the initial letters, the setup, the interviews before, what to say, what to do … He's really made that process his own. It helps too that the problems that the BMR throws up tend to be replicated again and again. But it's very much client-led the whole time. You're basically giving the client the tools to hand you back the solution.

And yet the process itself is revolutionary. I've heard client companies repeat that over and over: "Wow I thought I knew what consulting was about, but I've never been through a process like that before!"

A Note on Technology Support

The Odyssey Arrow is supported by an integrated client relationship management (CRM) system called Odyssey Quickstart, which is specifically designed to enable you to track contacts, activities, e-mail and other communications, resources, progress, and revenues/costs in each step of the Odyssey Arrow.

Chapter Summary

The Odyssey Arrow is the Odyssey business value development process. It provides practical, step-by-step guidelines showing how consultants move from identifying their Ideal Clients all the way through to delivering a Level 3 or Level 4 intervention. In this chapter, we covered the engagement practices in the Odyssey Arrow methodology. They are as follows: Executive Briefing (EB), Meeting One (M1), Meeting One Response Letter (M1r), Meeting Two (M2), and Business Management Review (BMR).

Before staging an EB, it is imperative to identify your Ideal Clients. The EB is then tailored to the specific needs of your Ideal Client base. The M1 is the first one-to-one meeting with the prospective client. It provides the platform to explore the possibility of further engagement with you. An extensive list of M1 questions is provided to facilitate a highly effective M1 meeting.

The consultant then follows up the M1 with the M1r. Its purpose is to capture the essence of your discussion at the M1, to give the client a deeper insight into the style and approach of your consulting business, and to make a recommendation on how the assignment/project can move forward.

The M2 and subsequent meetings help clarify the issues facing the company with other key staff members. The BMR is then arranged to provide the client with the forum to thoroughly explore all of the issues and challenges that the company faces.

Calls to Action

1. Using the exercise in this chapter, sketch your Ideal Client. Identify the client's sector, size, and characteristics. Consider what the Ideal Client is looking for, what kinds of interventions they will require, how they will find you, why they will seek your intervention, and how you will work together.

   _____

   _____

   _____

   _____

   _____

   _____

   _____

   _____

   _____

   _____

2. Identify three separate opportunities/partnerships/associations that could facilitate three separate EBs, targeting your Ideal Client base.

   _____

   _____

   _____

   _____

   _____

3. Develop an EB program outline using the following four key questions:
   a. What is your **promise?** One statement that captures the key benefit of attendance.

Sample: *We will provide you with an overview and key strategies for staying on your growth curve and achieving higher profitability and performance in your organization.*

_____

_____

_____

_____

_____

b. What is your **key message?** The statement that creates the call for the client to engage.

Sample: *All companies go through stages of growth. Today is an opportunity to critically examine where you are in your growth curve and identify what factors you are missing which WILL inhibit your future growth and KILL your profitability.*

_____

_____

_____

_____

c. What is your **offer?** What is the client take-away?

Sample: *We will provide you with a quick diagnostic to assess your "growth-curve killers" and a CEO road map to lead a "stages of growth" discussion with your executive team.*

_____

_____

_____

_____

_____

d. What is your **catch theme/title?** A short, commanding client attraction statement.

Sample: *Building a High Performance Company*
10 Critical Factors Killing YOUR Growth Curve!

_____

_____

_____

_____

4. Of, say, twenty people who will attend the EB, perhaps 20% may have some interest in having further discussions with you on a one-to-one basis. The EB will help them to verbalize a problem with recruitment or strategy, with succession planning or within the senior team. Explain how you will establish M1s with these clients based on first contact at the EB.

_____

_____

_____

_____

_____

_____

_____

_____

_____

5. Consider the M1 questions in relation to your prospective Ideal Client. Redraft all three sets of questions with particular reference to this client.

_____

_____

_____

_____

_____

_____

_____

_____

_____

_____

_____

_____

_____

_____

_____

_____

_____

_____

_____

_____

_____

_____

_____

_____

_____

_____

_____

_____

6. In relation to the same prospect, consider how many and what type of M2 and subsequent meetings will be required in the lead up to a full BMR.

_____

_____

_____

_____

_____

_____

_____

_____

_____

_____

7. Sketch a plan for a BMR for this client, bringing in the sample BMR setup e-mail and report contained in this chapter and adapting them to the particulars of your prospective Ideal Client.

_____

_____

_____

_____

_____

_____

_____

_____

_____

_____

_____

_____

_____

_____
_____
_____
_____
_____
_____
_____
_____
_____
_____
_____
_____
_____
_____
_____
_____
_____

Bibliography

Butler, J. (2000). *Successful Entrepreneurial Management: How to Create Personal and Business Advantage.* Dublin: Century Communications.

Czerniawska, F., & May, P. (2007). *Management Consulting in Practice.* Philadelphia, PA: Kogan Page Limited.

Larson, J. A. (2013). *Management Engineering.* Chicago: CRC Press.

Maister, D. H., Green, C. H., & Galford, R. M. (2004). *The Trusted Advisor.* New York: Simon & Schuster.

Maloney, T., & McLachlan, R. (2013). *Fortune's Impasse: Saving the Family's Jewels.* Burlington, ON: Newport Press.

Motles, S. (2014). *Reglas Mágicas Para Ser Un Líder Efectivo.* Santiago, Chile: Summit Consulting.

Niblick, J. (2013). *The Profitable Consultant: Starting, Growing, and Selling Your Expertise.* Hoboken, NJ: John Wiley & Sons.

Patterson, K., Grenny, R., McMillan, J., & Switzler, A. (2012). *Crucial Conversations Tools for Talking When Stakes Are High* (2nd ed.). Columbus, OH: McGraw-Hill Books.

Porter, M. E. (1985). *Competitive Forces.* New York: The Free Press.

Price, R., & Lisk, R. (2014). *The Complete Leader.* Eagle, ID: Aloha Publishing.

Chapter 3

The Odyssey Arrow Integration Phases: Delivering Strategic Imperatives

- What is the picture in your client's head?
- How well do you understand your client's total business?

We now consider the integration stages of the Odyssey Arrow. To repeat, the Odyssey Arrow is a visual representation of a discipline, a system, and a methodology with the ultimate objective of engaging with your Ideal Clients on key assignments to achieve masterful results. It gives the consulting process a series of well-defined, disciplined stages and corresponding actions that allow you to manage a consulting assignment in a controlled manner. The integration stages of the Odyssey Arrow begin with the Recommendation (REC), followed by the Organizational Development Intervention (ODI) and the Summary Evaluation Report (SER). To help illustrate the practice, we will continue to review Century Management's consulting engagement with ACP Engineering.

Recommendation

Laying the Groundwork for REC

The early stages of the engagement process, M1, M1r, M2, and BMR, provide the consultant with the in-depth knowledge of the business required to put them in

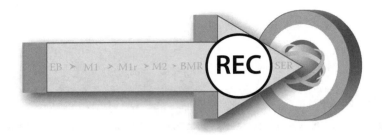

Figure 3.1 Recommendation.

a position to create a detailed REC tailored exactly to the needs and objectives of the client (Figure 3.1). Those initial stages also lay the groundwork for the essential buy-in within the company and serve to build trust, without which any intervention cannot succeed. An essential home truth here is this: The greater the team's involvement with the process, the greater the probability of its success.

Before issuing any REC, it is important that the core issues are clarified with the client, and thereafter that the objectives—both macro and micro—are documented and agreed upon. During that discussion, the issues and objectives should be stated using "native language"—that is, phrased in the client's own words—and placed in the correct order of priority by the client.

It is imperative that you are absolutely certain that you have a clear understanding of the client's perspective and the picture in their head before advancing to the next stage.

The Century Management Case Study

The REC document prepared by Century Management for ACP Engineering began by grouping the company's key strengths and the critical challenges they faced, as identified and stated in their BMR:

- ACP is ready to move forward.
- There is sufficient drive to change the culture throughout the practice.
- There is a lack of the critical core competencies that will be necessary to transform the practice.
- Not enough thinking time has been given to attitude management and business purpose.
- There is a requirement for a leadership process.

Flowing directly from these realities, the recommended intervention was broken down into macro and micro core objectives.

Macro Objectives

Creating Personal Leadership Awareness
    The aim here is to provide every staff member with the skills required to become a more effective team member.

Benchmarking the Competencies for Superior Performance
    Each role in the company will be benchmarked to identify the job-specific competencies required to carry out that role more effectively. In a parallel process, the person-specific competencies of each individual will be worked out, thus giving a clear indication of where the skills gaps lie.

Developing an Attitude of Personal Responsibility
    In addition, this element of the process will address the management of change through people, with an emphasis on interpersonal communication. Change management skills will be aimed at developing team building and improving overall performance.

Building a Shared Strategy for the Practice
    The aim here is to develop a shared strategy within the senior team, one which emphasises communication and business development. A vital part of the process involves transforming the management approach to one of strategic leadership. Developing a collective team identity and dynamic to promote greater collaboration and communication is also central to the overall improvement of the business.

Business Acumen
    The senior team must be equipped with the necessary knowledge and skills to build a leading-edge professional practice. To that end, we will explore business areas such as branding, marketing, consultative selling, and networking and financial areas, including fee setting and cash flow management.

Sustaining and Enhancing the Business Ethos and Culture at ACP
    A strong culture and team identity are essential to the growth and development of the business. Elements of ACP values and mission will be incorporated into business systems and processes, particularly in relation to performance evaluation.

Micro Objectives

Developing the Following Core Management Skills

- Interpersonal communications
- Effective communication techniques
- Emotional intelligence
- Coaching and facilitation styles
- Individual feedback
- Handling challenging work relationships
- Handling conflict
- Delegation skills
- Decision making
- Problem solving

The Recommendation

With key objectives defined, it was time to outline the intervention. Century Management recommended a four-phase integrated process. Although the phases themselves are distinct and self-contained, each one is also fully integrated into the process as a whole.

The coming pages feature selected extracts from the REC issued to APC Engineering. The overall aim was to achieve significant and sustainable change within ACP in the areas of personal and professional development, business management, and strategy formulation, and to ensure that the professional culture evolved as the business grew.

Internally branding the implementation process can help ensure buy-in and embed the intervention in the client company. Sometimes the client chooses a name of significance for the process. In other cases, they are happy to go along with a title and theme of our choosing.

In one case, we put the name "Rubicon Process" on the entire intervention. Senior management had a thorough immersion in the process, mid-level experienced a slightly lesser immersion, and the lower level participated in the lowest immersion. Everyone, however, participated in the "Rubicon Process." We liken it to serving larger slices of the pizza to senior management and smaller slices of the pizza to the other levels in the organization.

In this case study, for simplicity, we went with "APC" as the title of the process:

Phase 1: APC competency—communications and team building
Phase 2: APC business—the business of the professional practice
Phase 3: APC strategy—strategic thinking and planning
Phase 4: APC integration—follow up and follow through

Phase 1: APC Competency—Communications and Teambuilding

There are three main steps in Phase 1: APC Competency—Communications and Teambuilding. The TTI Success Insights portfolio of assessment solutions forms a valuable part of the competency REC.

Step 1: Setting the Context and Defining the Job-Specific Competency Requirements
The scene is set with the release of an announcement letter to everyone participating in the program. This is followed by an orientation briefing from the partners to help ensure buy-in. Key positions in ACP are then defined in terms of their job-specific competency requirements. The Century Management web-based system is then used to establish a benchmark for each of these positions.

Step 2: Measuring Each Individual and Highlighting the Key Competency Gaps
Each executive completes a personal talent exercise, which provides them with a document highlighting their natural and work-related behavioral styles, their motivational drivers, and their personal and leadership skills. After this process, members of the ACP team will get an individualized report indicating their capabilities and their specific learning requirements compared with the benchmark for that position.

Step 3: Delivering ACP Competency—Communications and Teambuilding
The purpose of Step 3 is to deliver a comprehensive learning and development process to all individuals, addressing professional competency and skills development, personal leadership development, teamwork, communications improvement, and change management. ACP Competency will be applied under the following headings:

■ Time management that gets results
■ Coaching and staff development

- Giving and receiving feedback as a communications process
- Developing responsibility and commercial awareness
- Developing a "standard professionalism" across the organization

Phase 2: APC Business—The Business of the Professional Practice

The primary focus of this phase is on marketing, selling, positioning, and building a profitable professional services business.

APC Business—The Business of the Professional Practice is designed to help the ACP senior management to develop an understanding of the difference between the profession of engineering and the business of engineering. This process will facilitate the recognition of paradigms that help build the business and those that hinder business success.

Phase 2 will focus on the following:

- Marketing strategies that work in a professional practice
- Value-based fees and fee setting methods
- Three overlapping essentials of high-income results-based professional services firms
- The repositioning paradigm mind-set
- Bad business is worse than no business; when to walk away; the causes of underpricing and all its implications
- How to use lateral vision in consultative selling with economic buyers
- Developing strategic selling and ROI selling as an integral part of your consulting engineering business
- The power of "pen" selling, war stories, and the concept sale
- Who are the big professional services firms? What do they do well, and how can you imitate their top performers to transform your business?

Phase 3: APC Strategy—Strategic Thinking and Planning

The Strategy Model is a seven-step system designed to enable ACP to create sustainable business advantage and to accomplish personal and business objectives.

The seven stages in the process are divided between the thinking steps and the planning steps.

The Thinking Steps

Step 1: Current situation analysis
Step 2: Writing up your history
Step 3: Clarifying and ordering your values
Step 4: The power of purpose … crystallizing your mission

The Planning Steps

Step 5: Commitment to a clear vision and critical success factors for the
next five years
Step 6: Writing clear strategic goals for next year and the year after
Step 7: Implementation—tactical planning

The purpose of the thinking part of the ACP strategy model is to discover innovative, imaginative strategies to create business advantage and successful futures for everyone. The planning part of the model is more operational and practically orientated. It is also more formal, conventional, and analytical. Taken together, the seven-step model provides a solid framework that embodies sufficient latitude and dynamism to adapt to change and make this document a living process.

The overall objective of the ACP strategy process is to create a long-term strategic advantage and to maximize the potential of all the resources in ACP at a time of great change. Everyone within the practice can refer to the ACP strategy document to facilitate the development of a culture that combines operational excellence with strategic clarity and focus.

The model keeps everyone involved and focused on achieving a successful outcome. Completion is critically important. Getting sidetracked and failing to complete the process leaves a vacuum that is invariably filled with cynicism and scepticism. It sends the message that the senior management is not sufficiently committed to the process to prioritize it.

The consultant's job in conducting this strategy exercise is to walk the line between pushing the process and giving enough time for discussion and dialogue. It is a balancing exercise that requires considerable skill. The amount of discussion and dialogue will be directly proportional to the ownership of and commitment to the final product.

When the process begins, it is primarily a communications, creativity, and team exercise. This is because most organizations already have the solutions to their own particular problems hidden in their capacity and knowledge base. The consultant's objective is to awaken those dormant solutions and help create the process that will bring them to bear on the client's business.

Phase 4: APC Integration—Follow Up and Follow Through

The APC Integration process is an integrated organization-wide program that needs an internal change agent and champion to ensure that it is implemented deep into the heart of ACP.

The role of this internal consultant/champion is vital to the long-term success of the ODI. They must take the ownership of the process within the company. This internal champion will need to be knowledgeable on all aspects of the business. This means that they will have to move from being a specialist to being a generalist.

Resistance, even cynicism, is part and parcel of a change process. Making resistance work for you is a key objective of the internal champion. Helping to get "early wins"—sometimes individual by individual—is another aspect of the role played by the internal champion.

Organizational Development Intervention

The ODI is the penultimate phase of the Odyssey Arrow consulting process. Having made a clear diagnosis and REC, the time has now arrived to make the assignment happen (Figure 3.2).

For the Odyssey consultant, the ODI stage provides you with the opportunity to leverage the strong, trusting relationship you have built with the client and demonstrate, at first hand, the practicalities of your expertise, intervention frameworks, change processes, solutions, and recommendations.

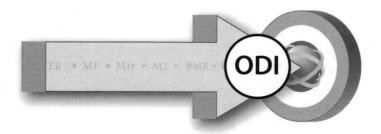

Figure 3.2 Organizational Development Intervention.

Client implementation is the fundamental purpose of any consulting assignment. Whether the problem is IT integration, identifying a new market opportunity, creating a learning organization or changing the organizational culture, the ultimate responsibility for implementation now transfers to the client.

Just as a doctor cannot force the patient to take either medicine or advice, your client must take responsibility for carrying out all of the steps and processes specified in the REC. This handover of responsibility is easier said than done and is best carried out in planned phases, depending on the complexity and context of the assignment. Being clear about the role the consultant plays in the client implementation stage is important for both parties.

Summary Evaluation Report

Once the assignment is completed, the final phase of the Odyssey Arrow is all about staging a successful exit. Having diagnosed, recommended, and implemented in a professional manner, the onus now lies with you, the consultant, to manage the disengagement in a planned, professional manner (Figure 3.3).

Both the client and the consultant need to be absolutely clear about the exit strategy; last impressions are often as important as first impressions. "Slow death withdrawal" or waiting for the client to send goodbye signals is unprofessional and serves neither party well.

Writing an SER outlining how the assignment has met its objectives is the essence of a professional exit. The client needs to know that a project was a success and to hear the words "Here is the evidence to justify the resources invested on the process." In essence, the SER is your statement of value provided to the client.

Human performance improvement interventions and cultural change management strategies are inherently difficult to evaluate, but that evaluation should not be disregarded by the consultant. A professional evaluation

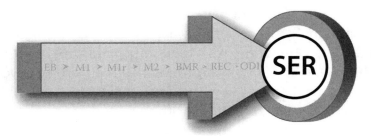

Figure 3.3   Summary Evaluation Report.

exercise, which indicates how a gap has been closed, how a cost has been eliminated, how time has been saved, how a sales metric has been increased, how an activity has been engaged in, or how productivity and profit have been improved, is the best way to close off the assignment.

The SER report outlines the outcomes and may suggest some ongoing recommendations as value-added advice or service for the client. The SER terminates the consulting assignment.

Odyssey in Action I

Ron Price, Price Associates, Boise, Idaho

It's Not a Product, It's a Partnership

I went through Odyssey in April of 2006. At the time, I had just started having a conversation with a company about a succession management project. Historically, in that context, I would automatically have thought of a product of some kind, a job benchmark or something of that nature, but because of my experience with Odyssey, I slowed down, I took a step back. I wanted to try to understand the significance of this project as it fitted into the big picture. So I flew out to meet with the CEO and his team. I spent half a day with them, and all but thirty minutes of that half-day was about listening to them, nothing more. I wanted to understand their situation. I wanted to operate on a much deeper level than I had ever tried to operate before.

I realized right away that I needed to get away from thinking about the specific details at the beginning—we can always get to the details later—I needed to step back and understand the big picture: What have they tried in the past, and if it didn't work, why didn't it work? What's the real impact of this particular issue? What's the emotional impact of this issue on the team? I realized that if I took the time to do all that and I wasn't anxious to rush out a proposal, I would develop a much better picture of what was going on. I would be able to help them see an opportunity not as a transaction but a transformation.

Towards the end of my time with them, I began to see what could be done with this client, and it was something that reached far beyond any particular product or workshop. They asked me, "Well, do you have any idea of what it would cost for you to help us with this?"

I told them that what they needed was not a product, it was a partnership. I said that I'd have to put pencil to paper, but my first thought was that the first project that they had identified might cost $250,000. It was the highest number I'd ever thrown out in front of a client. There was a two- or three-second hesitation, then the CEO said, "When can you get started?"

What happened next is revealing. When I did put pencil to paper and came back to them, I told them that the first element of the project wasn't going to cost $250,000 after all. It was only going to cost $155,000. Obviously, they were pleasantly surprised. I had just dropped my price by almost $100,000. Ultimately, however, that first intervention lead to a wide-ranging project that touched on many aspects of their business, and when all was said and done, they wrote us a check for 1 million dollars.

Odyssey in Action II

Tim Maloney, Newport Group, Ontario, Canada

The Smartest Person in the Room

This particular client came to an Executive Briefing of mine, and afterwards, he indicated that he was interested in what I was doing. He was a very busy prospect, with a net worth of maybe $60 million. So it took a little while to set up the M1. Accomplishing an initial meeting in this situation is all about walking the line between not appearing to be too available and accommodating, but facilitating the setup so that it can actually occur. Don't look up to or down upon any man is a thought I refer to often. My time is valuable, and I choose what I do with it. It's not available to others without me consciously or subconsciously projecting that it is. Say something like "When can we find a time that works for both of us?" Always let prospects volunteer a suggestion first. Value positioning starts early.

For me, it's important to establish a time window for the M1 upfront. A good M1 isn't a half-hour conversation, it's around ninety minutes to two hours but shouldn't be much more than that. It helps keep the focus on the prospect and off of yourself. While 90% of M1s are within that timeframe, if I see that a prospect is really engaged and that we are running out of time, I stop the conversation and say something like "It sounds like we have more to discuss than the time we originally allocated. This is important to you I think. I can take more time if you would feel that would be helpful." You gain agreement, then return to the conversation: "What were you saying about …?"

If you always take longer than two hours, before congratulating yourself on your conversational prowess, you may want to question your own preparedness and the questioning sequence that you are using. If your questions aren't general to specific, if they don't help your prospect move from fact, to logic and then emotional perspectives, you must rethink them.

Here's a suggestion to those of us who feel we have made it through life as reasonably bright human beings: It's not about you or how smart you are, or about how you have seen it all and have all the answers. Stop that, right now!

Don't sit forward on the seat, minimalize your body language; no dramatic nods or gestures are necessary. Ask questions, listen to answers, write notes, but only if you have asked permission to take notes, and don't ask until after you and the prospect have put the niceties behind you and they're settled into the conversation.

As indicated earlier, stick to generalities at first, but what you really want to do is to get to the point where the prospect's answers are moving away from his head and into his gut. You want a client to feel comfortable as they're talking; you want to hear why they got into their business, what the challenges are, what the company's got going for it ... It's a very easy process if you do it right and a very hard process if you do it wrong. A person can't fake genuine interest; never do that. Be genuinely interested in people and their ideas. As Zig Ziglar says, "Listening is not waiting for your turn to talk."

We met in Toronto. After an hour of going through all of the issues, he tells me, "My brother-in-law works for me and I had to fire him. I was paying him $200,000. Now I've got to pay severance of twice that, before tax ... And my sister's mad at me ..."

Believe it or not, things like this can have a huge impact on a business. It's those strange little things that cause people to take their eye off the ball. He's too busy worrying about how his sister is going to react to the fact that he canned her husband to deal with really significant business problems developing under his nose.

Of course, the other point here is that once a person has told you something like that, they'll pretty much tell you anything.

I'm really interested in three areas when I talk to a potential client. Firstly, what their revenue is and how it's trending. Second, what their payroll is and how that's trending. Third, what's their gross margin and how is that trending.

The reason I ask about these three things is that a lot of times, people say, "Well, we're doing more volume than we've ever done in the past. Sales are up!" what you tend to find however is OK, sales are trending up, but usually in that scenario, payroll is going to trend up because you're paying out more commissions, you're paying out more salaries. That's why I need to know gross margin. If sales are rising but gross margin is falling, you have a problem.

So this prospect was in that situation. Sales and payroll were up, but gross margin was down, and what's more, it was trending down. It had gone from 32% to 28% over the previous three years. If that trend continues in that exact same way, that prospect is going out of business.

At this point, I also ask some specific questions: What are revenues? What is payroll? What is margin today, and where do you feel it should be? How do you compensate your executive team? How much? What percentage of your overall payroll is tied up in executive salaries? Do you realize that is X% of your overall spend? Do you feel you get full value on the expenditure every year? Do you use gain share, profit sharing, or year-end bonus? How is that decided on? How is it measured? Has it shown measurable differences in the effectiveness of your payroll spend?

Once we have that kind of information, the questions change. You're moving a person from emotion back to logic, you're going back to the head from the gut. You start asking questions like: How much is this situation costing you? What are the ramifications if that continues? You're now beginning to monetize the situation with the client.

It turns out that this prospect has a $1 million per year problem. If he doesn't arrest the decline in his gross margin, he'll lose $1 million this year, $2 million next year, and so on.

At the end of the M1, I always say, "Thank you. It would be best for you if I go away and think about what you've told me. I have seen things like this before—not exactly your situation but certainly similar scenarios. I want to think about it. I'm going to get my thoughts down on paper, and I will send you back a letter."

That's the M1r, and in the response letter, you basically lay out some key quotes, just to show you were listening.

I hardly ever have an M2, unless the client wants to ask me a specific question. I'm going to suggest a BMR in the letter. Once the BMR is agreed, an appropriate fee is set, just for that initial stage. Resist any daydreaming with the client around what the actual fix will look like. Keep your powder dry. The fix will be discovered by the BMR participants. You don't have to do anything, but set them up to win and enjoy the process.

Any businessperson on the planet usually has about five or six people that they really count on to get things done. No one surrounds themselves with sixteen direct reports. These are the forward thinkers, and these are the people who are going to create the solution. I don't create the solution. I can provide a platform of competencies, processes, resources, and systems within which they create a solution, but the BMR group will create the solution itself.

I give each of these forward thinkers homework ahead of the BMR. They have to answer a list of questions about the business. These are very similar to the questions I've asked the owner by the way, but they do this as an individual exercise. They don't get together as a group; they actually write out their answers in advance of the BMR. That means they can't get together and fudge it. And it also creates what I call a collective vulnerability.

I pretty much know what I'm going to see every time. They will say we don't have enough communication, they will say there isn't enough role clarity, they'll say we're not getting enough performance feedback. These factors determine the level of trust in any organization. If you get these three right, you'll have a very trusting environment. If you don't, you won't.

At the BMR, I've got six or seven people in the room. They're senior people, they're well paid, they're all, as I say, collectively vulnerable. They've kicked themselves collectively in the ass for eight hours straight, and they're now in a zone where they're thinking, "We've got to fix this … We've got to move beyond where we're at. What are our priorities?"

At the end of the BMR, I always ask, "What does 'good' look like to you?" Once I know that, I can effectively ghostwrite the solution for my clients.

Intentionally, I don't spend much time thinking about what's going to happen—the Recommendation—until I have the right dynamic in place with the people who are going to benefit from whatever the solution is going to be. If you can save somebody a million dollars a year, you're worth a lot, so getting them to own the project that creates the solution is very important. Being the smartest person in the room and acting like you're the smartest person in the room in a consulting role is absolutely wrong. You've got to pull the solution from them. You've to encourage them to move forward.

Odyssey in Action III

Padraig Berry, ONEFocus, Dublin, Ireland

Slowing Down to Speed Up

I had actually started an engagement with this particular client *before* completing the Odyssey program in Ottawa. What it revealed to me is that I didn't really understand what I was doing.

Before participating in Odyssey, I had completed the equivalent of a BMR. I had thought that would tease out all of the issues, but it didn't. Why? Because I had missed out a couple of critical steps, particularly in relation to building the relationship with the CEO. I needed absolute clarity with him on what we were trying to do, and I didn't have that. I just didn't have it.

When I got back from Ottawa, I called up the CEO and told him that I wanted to stop the process. I explained that I didn't feel I fully understood the issues. I told him that I wanted to take a step back, that I wanted to "slow down to speed up," which is the expression that we use on Odyssey. I felt that the CEO and I were guessing our way forward, and I was very uncomfortable with that.

The CEO accepted all of this. So I began again, with the M1. I met him for a four-hour meeting and went through a comprehensive mind map of the M1 questions. I then went away and wrote a twenty-five page report—the M1r. All of this, I should say, was done pro bono. From an integrity perspective, it was vital that reinvigorating the process was not seen simply as an attempt to inflate the fees.

Ten days later, at the M2, we walked through the report line by line and agreed these were the critical areas, these were the real issues.

Before I restarted the process, I had never really addressed the CEO's personal vision. I had no clear idea of what he was trying to accomplish. I had no conception of the real issues because I had never asked the questions. Now, I was having that conversation.

We continued with the Odyssey Arrow and had the BMR. I compiled all of the information into a summary document then met the CEO again to go through it all.

The intervention we eventually decided upon was no longer a cost. It had become an investment. That too was really important to me from an integrity perspective. I felt certain that I was on the right track, that I could say things to him and recommend things to him with the utmost integrity. There was no issue of me trying to sell him anything.

He had originally talked about a €5,000 to €10,000 piece of work. The budget I proposed to him was €65,000, and I did that with absolute confidence. We could both see that this is exactly what he needed to do, and if he didn't do it, he would struggle. He accepted the figure without any argument.

Another point: Before the BMR, I had one-on-ones with each one of the executive team. I got their input about their goals and objectives, where they thought the company was going, what they thought the challenges were, and so on. Because I had those meetings, the team was much more forthcoming and much more willing to challenge the CEO during the BMR. They were able to say things like, "Well actually no, things aren't good, communications aren't fine ..."

I now have the confidence to charge fees that I would never have charged before, ever. I would never have had the courage to say, "That's a €65,000 piece of work."

Incredible though this seems, I now have next year's budget secured, and I secured it within a month of coming back from the Odyssey workshop in Ottawa and implementing the Odyssey Arrow. I've doubled my revenue from this year to next year. Anybody in the consulting field will understand what a result that is.

Odyssey has been a transformational experience for me. I now have absolute confidence that my business will grow and prosper. There is no doubt in my mind. This methodology is the only way to go, and I've been in this business for twenty-five years. I only wish I'd implemented it twenty-five years ago.

Chapter Summary

The integration phases of the Odyssey Arrow begin with the REC, which requires a thorough understanding of the client's issues and objectives driven by the M1, M2, and BMR. In the case example, the REC document issued to ACP Engineering began by stating the client's macro and micro objectives. The consultant, Century Management, went on to recommend a four-phased integrated intervention and implementation process (ODI), which embraced communications and team building, the business of the professional practice, and strategic thinking and planning.

The penultimate stage of the Odyssey Arrow is the ODI. Effective implementation requires a careful transfer of responsibility to the client company. A successful exit strategy using the SER is a vital element of that exit strategy.

Calls to Action

1. Using the concepts from this chapter, outline your portfolio of solutions and identify the kinds of interventions they are capable of addressing.

_____

_____

_____

_____

_____

_____

_____

_____

_____

2. What are the gaps or missing tools in your toolkit? Describe how you will address these solutions gaps.

_____

_____

_____

_____

_____

_____

_____

_____

3. Identify three separate opportunities where you can complete a total ODI intervention.

_____

_____

_____

_____

_____

_____

_____

_____

4. Map out your ideal value-based solutions and time frame for the coming six months … Who will you connect with? What is your recommendation? How will you measure success?

_____

_____

_____

_____

_____

_____

_____

_____

_____

_____

Bibliography

Behar, H., and Goldstein, J. (2007). *It's Not about the Coffee: Lessons on Putting People First from a Life at Starbucks*. New York: The Penguin Group.

Butler, J. (2005). *Successful Entrepreneurial Management: How to Create Personal and Business Advantage*. Dublin: Century Management.

Porter, M. E. (1998). *Competitive Advantage: Creating and Sustaining Superior Performance*. New York: Simon & Schuster.

Roam, D. (2009). *The Back of the Napkin: Solving Problems and Selling Ideas with Pictures*. New York: The Penguin Group.

Chapter 4

Applying a Client-Centered Value Strategy

- Are you creating the value dialogue with your client?
- Are you increasing your consulting market share?

In applying a client-centered value strategy, we examine how new techniques of consultative selling have radically altered the relationship between the client and the consultant. We also explore eight practical strategies for increasing revenues in your consulting business, discuss the consulting practice as a professional services firm, and take a look at the life and times of 400 consultants. We also examine six different consulting perspectives and explore ten options for intervening in the client organization.

Thoughts on Selling

In our work with consultants in our MasterClass, one of the key conversations we have is about selling.

"The word 'sell' bothers me," said one consultant. "As a professional, I really have difficulty with the idea of 'selling' my services. I like to say that I 'offer' my services."

It was a comment that pointed to a primary choke point for consultants who often believe that the client will automatically engage because the consultant has expertise, or a great process, a powerful change methodology or a unique engagement tool. Early conversations between a prospective client and a consultant tend to focus on Level 1 and Level 2 selling.

In life, most of our buying experience, good and bad, is conditioned in the realm of transaction selling. This experience creates a thought process we like to call "the mythology of selling." This mythology infects consultant thinking and manifests itself in many ways: short-term selling, fear of selling, selling on price, feelings of insecurity and failure. In the end, it may create a self-defeating prophecy where the consultant limits their opportunity to increase market share and to earn enough to create a profitable business.

Selling is part of the business of consulting. Selling at Levels 3 and 4 requires a process approach based on client needs and a mind-set shift on the part of the consultant.

Consultative Selling

Consultative selling is an indispensable discipline and strategy for success as an Odyssey consultant. It is a combination of persuasion skills, advanced communication, powerful influencing, and strategic insight. It is also a skill set that can be easily learned. Consultative selling, coupled with specialized knowledge and a code of ethics, is a Level 3 and a Level 4 methodology. At the heart of the process is the imperative to always act in the client's best interest. Consultative selling is relationship excellence in action. It is primarily focused on the potential client's experience during their interactions with you.

It is based on a win–win philosophy, where both client and consultant achieve value in equal measure. Consultative selling transcends the basic sales transaction and looks beyond it to nurture a long-term relationship. Consultants using consultative selling techniques ask more questions, listen actively, provide customized as opposed to generic solutions, interact through dialogue, and provide insights and education to potential clients.

Traditional Consulting Model versus Value Creation Model

The old model of generating revenues in a consulting business has changed dramatically during the last two decades (Figure 4.1). Clients have become more sophisticated, more knowledgeable, more equal to, and more sceptical of their professional advisors. That transformation has meant that the old

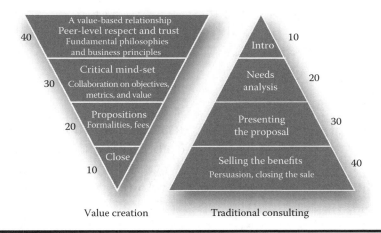

Figure 4.1 Value creation versus traditional consulting model.

ways of selling consultancy services are no longer fit for purpose. Traditional consulting was about an introduction (10% of time/effort), a needs analysis (20% of time/effort), a presentation on "what we will do for you" (30% of time/effort), and, finally, closing the sale with the benefits (40% of time/ effort).

The new model of consultative selling as embodied in the Odyssey Arrow is an inverted pyramid, with value creation as its core emphasis. It starts with developing and building peer-level respect. This incremental systematic process, outlined in earlier chapters, cannot be rushed.

The consultant must plan to move beyond Levels 1 and 2 transaction selling to become a Trusted Advisor to the client. Establishing a trusted relationship takes precedence over all other activities. It is about achieving a meeting of minds (and hearts) on fundamental business (and life) issues and root causes affecting the client's organization. This critical mind-set connection is confirmed as you collaborate on establishing objectives, metrics, and value outcomes.

Observe that these two steps (peer-level respect and trust + critical mindset) occupy fully 70% of the consultative process. Getting this right is fundamental to the model and to consultant–client success. Once a trust-based relationship is established and collaboration on metrics and value has begun, the process will fall into place naturally. The proposal is often a formality (20% of time/effort), and the close (10% of time/effort) is a logical conclusion to all that has gone before.

In summary, the trusting client engages you and your expertise first, your solutions second, and your company third. On the flip side, as an

Odyssey consultant, you must put the client first, your company second, and yourself third.

Our Story

When you are operating as a Level 3 Trusted Advisor, it is no longer about what you know or what you can do, it is about what the client wants. What are their objectives, dreams, and visions? You are not there to sell your products to the client; you are there to build a relationship based on trust and peer-level respect.

The great thing about the work that we do is we have a helicopter view into many businesses. We are not smarter than our clients; we just see more. When you are down in the engine room, utterly immersed in your business, it can be difficult to see the big picture and to see your business from a macro position to get the overall perspective. It is your role as a consultant to help your client take a step back and view the bigger picture and the overall business.

I took a call from a board member of a large hospitality industry company, a person with whom I had a long-standing relationship as a Trusted Advisor. He told me that the company had a problem with the senior management of their European division, and asked if I would travel to Europe to facilitate a workshop with the aim of resolving their problem.

In the traditional model of consultative selling, this would have prompted what I call "bag diving." The client gives you a line, "Oh, we're really bad at time management here," and this becomes your cue to sell a time management program. You dive into your bag and pull out the generic solution. However, when you are using the value creation model of consultative selling, you stop and ask the question, "Is this time management issue a symptom of something else?" You hold back and ask, "What's the full picture?"

When the client asked for a workshop to solve the issue with their European executive, rather than simply getting on a plane with my workshop materials in my bag, I sought more information.

I met with the board member, who told me about the problem executive in the European division. When he had finished talking, I said, "Here is a zero-based question: Knowing what you now know about that person, would you still hire him for that role?"

He said, "Yes, I think he's a good guy ... We just have a breakdown in communication."

I then needed to talk to the chief executive of the organization to understand the picture he had in his head and what he wanted to achieve. So I set up a meeting with him and talked with him for an hour and a half.

During that M1 meeting, I asked him the same question, "Knowing what you now know about this problem executive, would you still hire him for that role?"

He replied, "Absolutely not!"

I asked, "Would you hire this person for any role in the organization?"

He replied, "Absolutely not!"

So I asked him a few additional clarifying questions.

"What does the board say?"

"The board says get on with running the company."

"So what are you going to do?"

Having clarified his thinking and made his decision, he smiled and said, "You realize you're talking yourself out of a trip to Europe?"

"What's the point in me going over to Europe to run a workshop for someone who really shouldn't be in the organization?" I said. We both knew the answer.

The chief executive bit the bullet and put an exit package in place for the problem executive. When I met with him at the end of the year, he was in a much better place. There was a huge weight off his mind, and he was running a happier, more effective organization.

I was a Trusted Advisor to that CEO and his company. I had established peer-level respect and trust. In client engagements, I always ask myself, "What is the right thing to do here?" That was my question in this case. It is not about me getting a day's training; it is about what is right for the client. Your bag with its various solutions can be like a comfort blanket, to be wrapped around every issue the client presents. Moving to Level 3 Trusted Advisor and adopting the value creation consultative selling model approach means dropping the bag of solutions and going in naked—metaphorically speaking—without any preconceived solutions.

Ultimately, we were retained to conduct a senior management development process with the European division. The problem executive had already accepted his package and was working out his notice, but he asked if he could attend and participate in the program. During that program, he was one of the happiest people in the room. He had been miserable in his role. Taking that decision had relieved everyone of major stress and freed the person and the organization up to move forward.

I told this client my dentist story, which I like to recall when I sense procrastination in the decision-making process.

I had delayed going to my dentist because I do not much like the dentist's chair. On one occasion, my dentist asked me why I had taken so long to make the appointment. I told him that I did not like pain.

He responded with a profoundly wise statement, "You only prolong the pain by delaying the decision to come to the dentist." Point taken and lesson learned.

Eight Ways to Increase Your Consulting Revenues

Your survival in the consulting business depends on the generation of revenue, consistent cash flow, and profit. It is surprising how the word "profit" is frequently absent from the vocabulary of many consultants. The reality of course is that it is priority number one. The second related priority centers on how you allocate the money that comes into your business within that business, that is, admin, marketing, travel expenses, and so forth. That allocation determines your profit levels. It is critically important to have a good grasp of your financial well-being on a monthly basis. To grow your

Figure 4.2 Eight ways to increase your consulting revenues.

consulting practice, you must develop strategies that will address both revenue and profit growth (Figure 4.2). Here are eight ways to increase your
consulting business and market share:

1. Expand your client base.
2. Develop longer-term retainer-type contracts.
3. Create passive or parallel product income streams.
4. Broaden your strategic positioning.
5. Justify higher fees by creating higher perceived value.
6. Improve assignment profit margins.
7. Reduce the cost of client acquisition.
8. Develop strategic partnering relationships.

Expand Your Client Base and Attract New Clients

The first and most obvious way to increase consulting revenues is simply to
charge out more fees to similar kinds of clients as those you have at present.
It is vital, however, that the clients you identify are Ideal Clients, as discussed in Chapter 2.

Develop Longer-Term Retainer-Type Contracts

A great way to increase fees is to offer value propositions for extended periods of time. Explore the possibility of rescoping arrangements with existing
clients to a monthly, quarterly, or yearly basis. Think about what value you
can offer your clients for these extended contracts; are there recurring events
that provide opportunities here? Is the client experiencing particular problems that only longer-term solutions can solve?

Capitalize on Your Original Cost of Acquisition
by Creating Passive or Parallel Product Income Streams

Making product sales to your clients can have a double benefit, quite apart
from generating passive, additional income. Embedding tools in the client
organization keeps you in contact with them, something that frequently represents a challenge for consultants. Moreover, clients can easily forget good
work done for a client. Products such as assessments, books, and e-training
modules serve as a reminder of your value and provide a valuable "keep in

touch" mechanism once an assignment is wound up. Second, these products can act as high-impact marketing tools before a prospect becomes a client, for example, a free one-to-one assessment with a follow-up interpretation session.

Broaden Your Strategic Positioning: Sell Larger Assignments

Obtaining larger assignments—double, triple, quadruple, or even ten times your current contract size—automatically increases your revenues. Breaking out of Level 1 and Level 2 product-based assignments to Trusted Advisor level interventions is the essence of that expansion. Rather than simply selling time or a product, consider the scope for leveraging your existing relationship. Think about what you can change in your consulting business to obtain significantly larger contracts. The Odyssey Transformational MasterClass has seen several participants expand their strategic mind-set and service offerings.

Justify Higher Fees by Creating Higher Perceived Value

To justify higher fees to your client, you must increase the perceived value of your portfolio of solutions. Value is truly in the eye of the beholder. Your sales and marketing strategies together with your personal and professional branding are critical to positively differentiating your offering in the minds of your clients. Think about your image, your website, and your logo. Do these suggest to the client that you are a high-value proposition? Ask yourself what you have to change about who you are and what you do to significantly increase your charge-out fees.

Improve Assignment Profit Margins: Focus on Ideal Clients and Solutions

Many consultants tend to overlook the fact that profit is a normal part of the discourse of business and fail to include a profit margin in their fees. Maximizing profit margins and careful cash flow management are as important as increasing revenues if you are to achieve the ultimate goal of growing your consulting practice. Case by case, consider how to engineer a better profit margin from key assignments. The pricing of consultant expertise, know-how, and face time with the client organization is often overlooked. Do not neglect admin and fixed costs in calculating fees.

Reduce the Cost of Client Acquisition

How you invest your time, money, and energy in acquiring business from new or existing clients has a critical impact on the financial health and future prospects of your consulting business. Reducing the cost of client acquisition is frequently a function of positioning. Are you doing Executive Briefings (EBs) on a regular basis? Are you seeking ways to position yourself as a thought leader when you make presentations? Are you presenting to the right people? Critically assess your positioning process to see how you can better leverage your existing network. Avoid valueless association meetings. Evaluate on a cost/benefit basis whether social events simply assuage the ego and take your time but deliver little or no business opportunity.

Develop Strategic Partnering Relationships

Your expertise, processes, products, or methodology may be very useful to other consultants and professionals outside your field. For example, lawyers, accountants, venture capitalists, financial planners, and even banks encounter problems that require consulting analysis and expertise. These professionals do not provide these services but you do. Being on the on-call list is an opportunity to expand your consulting practice. EBs are an excellent way of getting the word out to potential partners about your services and creating a referral chain.

The Professional Service Firm

The term "professional service firm" used to refer solely to the regulated professions: accountancy, law, medicine, architecture, and so on. Over time, the definition broadened to include advertising agencies, investment banks, and consulting firms. Today, there are three aspects of the professional service firm that place the consulting business squarely within that definition.

Resource Base
Invariably, the consulting firm's resource base is narrow. It exists solely in the person of the consultant. The value of the consulting firm derives exclusively from the technical knowledge, expertise, and experience possessed by its professional staff. They are knowledge workers; their professional status derives from what they know.

Organizational Form

Similarly, the organizational form is often small, taking the form of a sole trader or a partnership with several contracted associates. The corporate model gives a much higher degree of autonomy than that which typically exists in conventional firms, and may be optimized to deliver strategic and tax advantage.

Professional Identity

This is a vital component of any consulting firm and captures the firm's brand, its presence, how it communicates, its tone, and the very essence of what it does. Your professional identity reflects the reality that when the client retains your services, they are essentially buying you. They understand, through that identity, that you have the expertise and the presence to provide the services that they need.

Distinctiveness of Professional Service Firms

The consulting business is not like other businesses. Consultants do not sell standardized products or services. To achieve results for their clients, they must develop customized solutions, which are then delivered by highly talented professionals. The consulting firm differs in its focus, not on volume or transaction but on delivering the optimal portfolio of solutions to its client base.

Although conventional businesses and consulting businesses may differ as discussed, there is one way in which they are identical. They both exist to generate profit. In the context of a highly personalized business, it is easy to lose sight of this fact. Consultants frequently place too much emphasis on revenue generation, without focusing on the vital role of profit in their business. If you are unable to quantify your profit in consulting, it begs the question, Do you actually have a business?

The reality of course is that consulting has become a highly profitable business, and as a result, it is growing rapidly. During the last ten years, consulting has grown by 16% per annum to become a $120 billion industry. There are currently in excess of 1 million consultants plying their trade across the globe.

It is estimated that the big players in the industry divide half of that $120 billion among them, with the remaining $60 billion spread among smaller firms and independent consultants. Although the charge-out fees of those one million consultants averages out at $120,000 per annum, the reality of course is that fee levels vary widely within the industry. Typically, however, research suggests that the 80:20 rule applies; 20% of consultants earn 80% of the revenues.

Although revenues do not determine profit levels on their own, they remain the predominant factor in profitability. It is vital in your consulting business that you are able to expose the relationship between the two, to be able to say, "I did X dollars in revenue this month, and I have a profit of Y."

The Life and Times of 400 Consultants

A survey conducted at the TTI Success Insights International Consultants Conference in Phoenix, Arizona, turned up some very revealing information about consultant revenues and lifestyle. In the anonymous questionnaire, we set out to determine how much consultants were earning, how they earned it, and why they did what they did.

Here are the six questions and the answers given:

What were your personally generated revenues as a consultant last year?
   Note that the question zeroes in on personally generated revenues as opposed to revenues earned by the corporate entity. In total, that single auditorium of 400 consultants generated revenues of more than $86 million the previous year. That is an average of $216,000 per consultant. Within that, the range of fees varied as you would expect. One consultant took home $1.3 million, whereas at the other end of the spectrum, a new entrant to the industry earned just $10,000. It is worth noting that eleven consultants—3% of the group—had revenues in excess of $1 million.

What was your biggest single fee last year?
   The biggest single fee in the auditorium was $600,000, the lowest was $10,000, and the average was $55,000.

How many years have you been in the consulting business?
   The average number of years in the business was 10.3. One consultant in the auditorium was looking back on thirty years in the business, whereas one newcomer had only been in consulting for a single year.

What age are you now?
   The average age was fifty-three years, with the oldest seventy-four years and the youngest twenty-three years.

How many car miles and air miles did you clock up last year?

Consultants frequently gauge their status by the mileage that they clock up. In terms of time spent behind the wheel, the average consultant drove 15,000 miles the previous year, although one hit a high of 80,000. The lowest was zero. The auditorium spent an average of 33,000 miles in the air, with a high of 300,000 air miles and a low, again, of zero. Best practice would suggest that your best client should be within half an hour's reach, to keep your time focused on the business of consulting rather than the act of getting there.

In one word, sum up your reasons for being in the consulting business.

This statement, which the consultants were asked to answer quickly and instinctively, is perhaps the most revealing of all. In order of the most frequent responses, the ranking is as follows:

1. Passion—being of service and making a difference to business and sharing wisdom gained
2. Freedom—freedom from the corporate world to enjoy greater balance and harmony and control of one's life and business
3. People—wishing to contribute to the growth and success of people
4. Fun—the opportunity to engage with many different kinds of businesses and people
5. Money—return on investment of time, knowledge, and experience, or simply cannot afford to retire
6. Helping—the sense of fulfilment from helping others achieve success

These figures, although they may surprise you, are consistent with global research into this area. Before you go on, think about why you joined the consulting business. What drives you to fulfil your dreams and maximize your potential?

Six Consulting Perspectives

The rapid growth of the consulting industry in recent years has seen a dramatic expansion of the scope and nature of consulting business models. As a result, it is important to understand these changing dynamics and be aware of the differing definitions that exist. The Odyssey approach encompasses six separate perspectives of consulting:

Perspective 1: The Generalist and the Specialist

"To be a generalist or a specialist, that is the question."

The dichotomy between the generalist and the specialist represents a common dilemma at the heart of consulting. You find specialists at all levels of the corporate structure: industrial engineers, financial analysts, and experts in a variety of disciplines. The management consultant, however, is not understood to have a comparable specialization.

The argument runs that generalists lack the in-depth knowledge required to fully understand and resolve problems, and provide little added value to the client business. Your clients will add fuel to this debate by implicitly or explicitly expecting that you be both a generalist and a specialist. The reality is that the strategic objectives of an organization in this fast-changing world require both generalists and specialists or a combination thereof.

For the consultant, the dilemma is that the more specialized your approach, the more difficult it is to obtain sufficient business, and the more generalist your approach, the less credibility you carry in the eyes of your client. The Odyssey consultant's position is as a generalist, but as a specialist within a niche market.

Specialist or technical consultants tend to focus on business processes, structures, systems, and technology in areas such as production, construction, legal, finance, and accounting. The generalists tend to focus on the human side of organizations, such as personal development, cultural change, strategic leadership, and energizing and empowering people to performance improvement.

Although you may be a generalist in your field, your clients need to perceive and believe that you are a specialist in their area of need. Imagine yourself as a zoom lens, capable of taking the broad approach but retaining the ability to zero in on your own particular area of competency and the specific need of the client sitting in front of you. In a generalist position, the consultant initiates the Odyssey Arrow and recommends a variety of solutions, some of which may require other niche consultant expertise. You become the coordinating consultant. For example, you might consult on human resource matters, but bring in a finance or technology consultant to implement other Recommendations.

Perspective 2: Business or Profession?

Is consulting a business or is it more accurately described as a professional service? Disciplines like medicine, law, accounting, and engineering have evolved into professional services over many years, during which the vocational characteristics and competencies that separate the certified professional from the business aspects of their activities have become clearly defined and generally accepted.

For consulting, the boundaries are less clear. Some would say consulting is a discipline, not yet a profession. At the same time, consulting is evolving rapidly, extending its reach deep into those more established professions.

The reality is that your consulting business coexists very nicely with your professional expert method of practice and service delivery. It is vital to maintain that dual focus and to understand that while you are providing a professional service, you must also operate a viable business. It is not credible to advise on the running of other businesses if you do not run your own business successfully.

The central question then becomes, How do I take a professional approach to management consulting, while at the same time making sure I build a solid, profitable consulting practice? Odyssey consultants subscribe to a code of ethics and strive towards a competency benchmark, while the Odyssey Arrow guides protocol and processes.

Perspective 3: The Nature of Consulting

Although there are several definitions of consulting, it is helpful to think of two basic contexts.

The first context is a broad, functional approach. Fritz Steele (1975) in *Consulting for Organizational Change* defines it as follows:

> Consulting is any form of providing help on the content, process, or structure of a task or series of tasks where the consultant is not actually responsible for doing the task itself, but is helping those who are.

In his book *Flawless Consulting: A Guide to Getting Your Expertise Used* (2011), author Peter Block states,

> You are consulting any time you are trying to change, or improve a situation, but have no direct control over the implementation. By this definition, many executives in organizations are really consultants, even if they don't officially call themselves consultants. So, if

you are a helper, or an enabler, or a provider, or even a manager, you can assume the consulting role.

Consulting, therefore, is open-ended in nature, and far from being the preserve of an elite, it is available to anyone wishing to "hang out their shingle." This availability helps to explain the application of the title "consultant" to everyone from sales consultants to IT consultants and public image consultants. In its broad definition, consulting is an approach or a way of advising or telling others to do something they might not have done, or improving on something they are already doing, and most likely charging a fee for service.

The second context of consulting views it as a specialist profession with several clearly defined characteristics. In *Consulting to Management* (1983), Greiner and Metzger state,

> Management consulting is an advisory service contracted for and provided to organizations by specially trained and qualified persons who assist, in an objective and independent manner, the client organization to identify management problems, analyze such problems, recommend solutions to these problems, and help, when requested, in the implementation of solutions.

The International Council of Management Consulting Institutes (ICMCI) defines consulting as follows:

> Management consulting is the provision of independent advice and assistance about the process of management to clients with management responsibilities.

The late Peter Drucker (2001), management guru, states,

> Every consultant knows that his clients are his teachers, and that he lives off their knowledge. The consultant does not know more. But he has seen more.

In Odyssey, we believe the primary role of consulting and the consultant is to create, share, and apply management and business knowledge, methodology, and processes for the benefit of the client. Although knowledge transfer is a key aspect in consulting, consultants have the practical experience to add value to the assignment. They stay within the boundaries of what they know, what they can do, and the results they are able to deliver. They call on other consultants with the requisite knowledge, skills, and experience to augment the assignment as required.

Perspective 4: Consulting Is Always Temporary

At its simplest, consulting is about entering into the client organization, carrying out an assignment, and getting out. Despite the harshness of the definition, it does accurately capture the reality that consulting should have a clearly identifiable end. This is a reality that insecure consultants frequently disregard, fearing the loss of guaranteed remuneration. They latch onto a client company and find reasons not to let go. They forget that professional service is assignment driven. By their very nature, assignments have three stages: a beginning, a middle, and an end. The consultant must define each of these stages and make an honorable exit.

Perspective 5: The Purpose of Consulting

We outlined how Odyssey views the role of the consultant in a professional context in Perspective 3. This perspective explores the Odyssey purpose of consulting and how it shapes the approach to client assignments. Odyssey aims to capture the underlying motives of assisting and advising that permeate all of the definitions of consulting we have met so far.

Odyssey defines the purpose of consulting as follows:

Management consulting is a professional and business advisory service that assists clients to achieve their strategic objectives by

- Helping solve management and business problems and challenges
- Identifying and taking advantage of new opportunities
- Embracing talent management and "the learning organization"
- Assisting and advising on the implementation of change
- Creating tangible and intangible value for the organization

The primary purpose of Odyssey consulting lies in helping clients articulate and achieve their major purpose, their "magnificent obsession," along with their vision, mission, values, and critical strategic imperative(s). The Odyssey consultant's purpose is to bring objective focus, clarity, and capacity through the Odyssey Arrow.

Perspective 6: How Do Consultants Intervene?

Here, we delve deeper into consulting to explore the flexible nature of the discipline and to examine the ten options that are available to consultants intervening in client organizations.

Information Gathering

Information is the raw material of all knowledge-based industries. One of the most basic interventions a consultant makes in a client organization is data gathering. They study and gather information, collate it, and use it to deepen their understanding of the organization and its needs. As an independent third party, the consultant is able to dissect, discern, summarize, and report on this information in an objective manner.

Specialist Services Provider

The consultant is frequently a specialist services provider, sent in to perform a particular task or manage a project, carry out a hiring assignment, perform project appraisal, review systems or manufacturing specifications, or to provide independent third party advice.

Networking Management

The consultant often has the capacity to move laterally and vertically within a client organization. You might begin with the CEO and obtain a referral to human resources, or you might begin at a lower level in the organization and progress to the CEO's office. Invariably, this mobility gives the opportunity to connect with many individuals and teams in the organization, creating additional revenue opportunities.

Sounding Board/Mentor

The consultant often acts as a sounding board for management or, moving up the ladder, for the board of directors. Results-based solutions and change opportunities are identified and explored with the client, regardless of what position they occupy within the hierarchy. This role might dovetail with that of the mentor or executive coach.

Research and Diagnosis

Closely related to the information gathering intervention, research and diagnosis is a good starting point for the consultant to engage a client organization. It is important that the consultant has an appropriate level of research skill, certification, and tools to initiate and implement diagnostics and surveys. The consultant's validated research findings and objectivity provide the independence that is necessary to identify the sources of problems and determine solutions to those problems while building value.

Implementing Proposals

An external consultant perspective can also be beneficial to the successful implementation of proposals with a client. Again, the consultant brings independence and a fresh perspective and is untainted by the legacy issues that can otherwise make change implementation problematic in the client organization.

Developing Systems and Methodologies

In developing new systems and methodologies, the consultant brings their experience of other projects to bear with the current client. Whether it is the formulation of a performance management system, a process control system, or assisting in creating an onboarding process, this is one of the most common interventions managed by a consultant.

The Change Agent

As an Odyssey consultant, it is vitally important to understand the anatomy of change and have a working knowledge of change strategy. Consultants deployed as change agents need a clear understanding of the ways in which change affects an organization and its employees.

Human Performance Improvement

This is all about the analysis and assessment of people and processes, the identification of performance gaps, and the formulation of interventions to close identifiable gaps, along with the creation of systems and processes to sustain performance and productivity.

Executive Coaching

A consultant will often enter the organization as an executive coach, invited to provide senior management with one-on-one guidance and backup to assist them to be more effective in fulfilling their roles. It is in this capacity that the Odyssey consultant has the greatest opportunity to progress to Trusted Advisor status. Coaching leads to consulting, and consulting leads to coaching.

Odyssey in Action I

Mel Nelson, President & CEO, Executive Management Systems,
Fargo, North Dakota

Letting the Client Lead the Way

I did an EB on June 19. I had a pretty good audience, made up of business owners and CEOs. Afterwards, I had a chance to sit with one of these men over lunch. I knew we had a connection instantly. Building the relationship is such a key part of this process, and you do it right off the bat, right from the Executive Briefing, long before you have the first meeting.

I've always maintained that if you don't have chemistry with someone, you can tell very quickly. One of the things that we need to do as Master Practitioners is have a high-speed taxiway, an off ramp, where a plane can get off the main runway quickly. That off ramp is the way we de-select unsuitable clients. If the client is never going to leave the ground, it's important to abort early and get off the runway. They are wasting our time when we need to get other payloads into the air.

I shared the four levels of consulting model with this client—the Good Soldier, the Competent Warrior, the Trusted Advisor and the Master Practitioner—and I could tell that we were developing a solid rapport, that he would remain on the runway, preparing for takeoff.

I think of the Value Creation Pyramid in terms of results-based, talent-driven consulting. The first level of that pyramid is peer level respect and trust, and this is the key.

From that EB, which took place on June 19, through September 2—Labor Day weekend—we had no contact, but I had made up my mind that I was going to follow up with this individual. I ran into him that weekend, and I mentioned a particular area of need that he had identified during our earlier conversation. I suggested he come to another briefing that I thought he might find interesting. He said, "Great, but let's talk next week."

So we talked that Tuesday. As far as I was concerned, I was taking things slowly, talking through the issues, building rapport, creating trust, and developing a relationship. I was still in the same zone of the pyramid. Then, all of a sudden, he said, "Are you interested in a business proposition?"

He just went right to the heart of it. As far as he was concerned, trust had been established, and peer level respect was there. It was the client—not me—who prompted the move to the next level, the takeoff. No need for the high-speed off-ramp.

The second level of this inverted pyramid is collaboration—creating the critical Mindset. That's where we got on board with the M1 meeting.

Afterwards, I prepared the M1r letter, which was about twelve pages long, detailing both his thinking and the value I could bring to the table. He told me that he spent 45 minutes reading that letter. When do you get an executive to spend 45 minutes reading a piece of correspondence?

One of the things that is so powerful in this whole Odyssey Arrow process is when you give them back their words and their thinking. It's like holding up a mirror to them. They're seeing elements of their complexion that they've never seen before. They're going places they've never gone before because you've built that trust.

Now, the third level of this pyramid is the proposition, defining the engagement. You've built the critical Mindset, now you're defining the engagement. Because of the trust that's been built up, this becomes a very powerful part of the discussion.

Within five weeks of that Labor Day encounter, I was meeting with him and his leadership team in Phoenix for a day-long BMR. I've got a three hour meeting with him scheduled next week where we're going to do a deep dive into the concepts that came out of that BMR.

Even though we're still at a relatively early stage of the Odyssey Arrow, I know that this is going to be a significant engagement. I am confident that it's going to run between five and seven years and that it will be on multiple levels. It will happen, and it will happen not only because of the breadth of services that I can bring to the table, but by the fact that trust and peer level respect have been established.

Odyssey in Action II

Jean Ann Larson, Managing Partner, Jean Ann Larson & Associates, Dallas, Texas

Building a New Consulting Business

I came from the healthcare industry and worked internally as a consultant in the leadership and talent management space. After thirty years, I decided to go out on my own. Like so many new consultants, I knew my stuff, but

I didn't really know how to go about turning it into a business. That's what brought me to Odyssey.

I had hit that early stage consultancy dilemma. You want to chase sure earners, and you're tempted to get every small job going, but really what you need is to develop relationships and embed yourself more deeply in the client organization.

As another Odyssey consultant pointed out to me, when you go in as Trusted Advisor, you don't have to chase fifty or sixty customers, because you're going to provide more value to and generate more revenue from the small number you have a relationship with. And that relationship will generate additional business. What's more, it plays to my strengths, and it's a lot more fun working with clients on that level, as opposed to just selling products and chasing those small jobs.

The healthcare sector tends to be dominated by not-for-profit organizations, and that fosters an attitude that there's never sufficient resources to pay you for your services. I had to get really clear on the fact that I'm not just selling stuff, I'm providing value. It was very easy for me to sell myself short, to start deep-discounting because I was new. My Odyssey mentor was like, "Snap out of it Jean Ann. You're a powerful consultant. Here's what you should charge, and not a penny less." I did what she suggested and the client didn't even blink.

I found too that if you do a good job at the right level, the client takes you with them. It's amazing how quickly people jump from company to company, from job to job. That's your advantage as a consultant because if you work with a client and suddenly they're somewhere else, it opens up a new line of business for you.

I've been very active in staging EBs as a means of bringing in new clients, but my big "aha" was this: Unless I'm in front of the right group of people who'll bring me in at the right level for the right purposes, I'm just an entertainer.

In the same vein, I pushed some of my networking groups aside. They're great fun. I've met great people and had great lunches—I live in Dallas and people love to go out to lunch—but what I've found is that none of this activity results in business. So I've had to become a little more mercenary and think, is this just a transaction or is this a relationship that's going to lead to something?

The other side of that coin is you have to be patient. Relationships take longer than transactions. I may start talking to someone and months later we finally have a conversation that may result in business. People have to get to know me; how can I become a Trusted Advisor if they don't appreciate who I am and what I'm doing.

I'm also building passive streams of income, through writing books, writing articles, and developing e-courses. In addition to the income, these activities get my name out there and help to establish me as an expert.

While some of the networking groups haven't delivered, I do have one networking group which has been instrumental in giving me the confidence to go for bigger jobs, because it's made up of experts whom I can bring into client interventions as partners. That's one of the great things about Odyssey. It gives me a pool of other consultants that I can go to when I want to bid for projects that I couldn't do on my own.

Chapter Summary

Many consultants have difficulty with the words "sell" or "selling." However, selling is part of the business of consulting. Selling at Levels 3 and 4 requires a process approach based on client needs and a mind-set shift on the part of the consultant.

The Value Creation model of consultative selling inverts the traditional consulting approach by emphasizing the primacy of relationship building. Once peer-level respect and trust are established, the critical mind-set facilitates collaboration on objectives, metrics, and value. Proposition and close then follow as a natural conclusion. In the Value Creation model, the client is not sold a commodity; they make an investment in their business.

Because this process is founded on doing what is best for the client, "bag diving" or simply providing the client with the most obvious solution is not always the best or most credible course of action. The Odyssey Arrow facilitates an effective consultative selling process that delivers value for the consultant and the client.

Although the needs of the client are at the very heart of the consulting practice, it is also vital to remember that you want to run a profitable consulting business. The eight ways to increase your consulting revenues demonstrate practical methods of remaining client centered while growing your consulting practice.

The survey data taken at a TTI Success Insights conference in Phoenix, Arizona, reveal a great deal about consultant lifestyle and revenues.

Odyssey embraces six perspectives of consulting, each of which helps to illustrate the consultant's functional role as a powerful third party within the client organization.

Calls to Action

1. Using the concepts from this chapter, review the strategic changes you could make in your business to capture longer-term client assignments.

_____

_____

_____

_____

_____

_____

_____

_____

_____

_____

2. What can you do in the next ninety days with new or current clients to increase your fees? What percentage increase in net profit will you achieve?

_____

_____

_____

_____

_____

_____

_____

_____

_____

3. Outline what you have to change with regard to who you are and what you do to significantly increase your charge-out fees?

_____

_____

_____

_____

_____

_____

_____

_____

_____

4. What do you need to do more of to reduce the cost of client acquisition? What do you need to do less? Be specific.

_____

_____

_____

_____

_____

_____

_____

_____

_____

5. Focusing on profit margin, review each of your clients in turn. Which kind of project affords you the best chance of profit improvement?

_____

_____

_____

_____

_____

_____

_____

_____

_____

_____

Bibliography

Butler, J. (2010). *Business Model Innovation: Proven Strategies That Actually Work.* Sevierville, TN: Insight Publishing.

Drucker, P. (2001). *The Essential Drucker.* New York: HarperCollins.

Greiner, L., & Metzger, R. (1983). *Consulting to Management.* Englewood Cliffs, NJ: Prentice Hall.

Hanan, M. (2004). *Consultative Selling: The Hanan Formula for High-Margin Sales at High Levels* (7th ed.). New York: AMA Publications.

Lippitt, G., & Lippitt, R. (1986). *The Consulting Process in Action.* San Francisco: Jossey-Bass/Pfeiffer.

Steele, F. (1975). *Consulting for Organizational Change.* Boston: University of Massachusetts Press.

Weiss, A. (2011). *The Consulting Bible: Everything You Need to Know to Create and Expand a Seven-Figure Consulting Practice.* Hoboken, NJ: John Wiley & Sons.

Chapter 5

The Business Behind Consulting

- What is your level of business financial knowledge?
- Which factors in your business are limiting cash flow and profits?
- How do you price your service and solutions to reward your talent?

Financial Intelligence

In a nutshell, financial intelligence is the ability to generate sufficient cash flow and profit to meet your business and life goals. It is all about ensuring that every cost is managed, investing profits wisely, and not losing sight of the key metrics that drive the health of your business.

Despite the critical nature of this financial arena, it is one that consultants all too frequently ignore. The core reality is that the ultimate barometer of the success of your consulting business is profitability. Every activity within that business must contribute to a specific profit amount, directly or indirectly. Your primary aim is to generate profits to achieve the greatest possible return on your time, energy, and invested capital.

Ask yourself this question, If I am not working on and generating profit in my business, how am I qualified to talk about profitability of the client's business?

In this chapter, we look at ways of assessing the metrics that govern profit and examine fee setting and the primacy of results-based consulting.

Critically, we demonstrate how to shift your thinking to generate higher fees and drive greater profitability.

The Odyssey Profit Drivers

A profit driver is a specific focus point where you exert direct action to achieve a profit advantage. Profit drivers have a multiplier effect on profit; they punch way above their weight (Figure 5.1). A small change to a profit driver can dramatically improve your chances in a competitive situation. There are six profit drivers:

- Staff
- Personal
- Client
- Sales and marketing
- Solutions
- Market

Figure 5.1 The Odyssey profit drivers.

Together, these drivers form a chain, and as with any chain, one weak link can damage or even destroy your entire consulting business. However, the converse is also true. Eliminating one profit-limiting factor creates a ripple effect across your practice, improving all other processes and systems in your business.

Most consultants do not know how to look for the weak links in their practice. In this chapter, we discuss ways to review and assess your practice to zero in on critical weaknesses in your business and financial systems. You will find that strengthening the weakest profit link will be among the most significant financial interventions you will make in your business this year. You may also want to seek the advice of your accounting and finance consultant to review your financial model and systems.

Staff Profitability

Payroll is always the largest expense in any consulting practice. When calculating payroll costs, many independent consultants pay themselves either poorly or last and justify this by telling themselves that the big payoff will come later. This is simplistic thinking.

Put yourself in the business owner category rather than in the self-employed category. All staff, including you, must yield an acceptable rate of return. Better still, each staff member should contribute a maximum return on investment (ROI).

In the professional services industry, the "one third, one third, one third" rule tends to apply to allocation. One third of revenues goes towards profit, one third applies to the delivery of your services, and one third covers administration costs. Let the following questions guide your thinking in relation to staff profitability:

- Who is not paying for themselves?
- What will you do about this?
- What can you do with staff who are not producing optimum returns?
- What is your process for hiring staff?
- How do you pay yourself?

High staff costs can be reduced by hiring on short term contracts, working with a virtual assistant and sharing staff resources with other small organizations.

A Consultant Danger Zone

Consultants in early start-up mode tend towards creating partnerships prematurely. Partnering is often a result of the need for "consulting comfort" and the "thought euphoria" associated with one's newfound freedom to sell expertise and services. If not structured appropriately, however, these partnerships can become time consuming, unproductive, and costly for all involved. Your time may be better deployed by focusing your energy on looking for clients and creating your brand of leadership. A more rewarding support strategy may be to contract expertise as required. Productive partnerships evolve when you have an established practice identity, which attracts those with like mind, ethics, and heart.

Personal Profitability

Your personal rate of return is the single most important contributor to your overall success. Your ability to consistently earn an above average income is your most valuable asset. Time is the critical resource. How you use the 168 hours available to you every week will determine your revenues and profits.

A good question to make a habit of asking yourself regularly is, what am I doing at *this* moment that is contributing value to my business? You should be able to quantify your answer using cash flow and profitability variables. The time will come when summer will ask, "What have you been doing all winter?" Or winter will ask, "What have you been doing all summer?"

The only time an Odyssey consultant should think about an hourly rate is when calculating costs on how much time to allocate to key productivity, performance, and administration tasks on a project/proposal basis. This exercise is for your own internal use to establish a preliminary project profit/loss analysis to determine the overall project fee to be submitted to the client in the Recommendation (REC).

Value Basics

Let us say you work 2,000 hours per year. Now, divide that figure into your annual net income and you get your hourly rate. Let us say you pay yourself $100,000 per year. Divide by 2,000, and you arrive at an hourly rate of $50.

Once you have established that critical figure, you must take action. Stop doing administrative low-value tasks that can be completed by someone else for less than $50 per hour. You must outsource, delegate, or eliminate any tasks that do not give you the maximum return on your time.

Doing the wrong thing well is the height of folly. By continuing to carry out tasks that can be done less expensively by someone else, your business is incurring an opportunity cost, thereby damaging your revenues and your overall profitability. Level 1 and 2 consultants often unconsciously fall into the habits of being a Jack or a Jill of all tasks and a master of none.

One of our graduates told me recently, "I suddenly realized how much unproductive time I was spending on social media, thinking it was going to generate business. I was deceiving myself. It was event management at its worst. What I needed to do was to get busy working on a powerful Executive Briefing that I could deliver in my immediate business community."

Consider how much time you spend on the critical success factors (CSFs) of a profitable consulting practice.

■ What is the one thing you need to *stop* doing in terms of personal productivity?
■ What do you need to *start* doing immediately in terms of personal productivity?
■ What are your CSFs? How much time are you spending on them?
■ What are the critical number of CSF's you need to focus on all the time?
■ How can you save 15% of your costs for the next 60 days?

Client Profitability

Client profitability is the relationship between the fees you charge and the time you spend on the assignment. Some clients may be very profitable; others may actually be costing you money. The 80/20 rule frequently applies: 20% of your clients contribute 80% of your profits.

The question then becomes as follows: What do you do with your least profitable clients, who still absorb your time and your talent? Creating the time to find your Ideal Client is often the most neglected priority for a consultant. Do not fall into the trap of confusing being busy with doing good business.

■ Which clients do you need to let go?
■ Identify two Ideal Clients you will work to get on board in the next six months.

Sales and Marketing Profitability

Money spent on sales and marketing is often perceived as a cost. The reality is that sales and marketing is an investment, and as such, you need to know the impact not just on revenues but on profits.

A proven sales and marketing investment is the delivery of well-thought out, well-organized, and well-executed Executive Briefings.

In a small consulting practice, it is relatively easy to track spending to arrive at that ROI figure. For example, you can measure the direct costs involved in organizing four Executive Briefings per year, which will involve targeting some 300 Ideal Clients or prospects in your locality. The key questions then are all about your markets:

- What markets do you need to exit?
- What market research is required to identify your Ideal Clients?
- What markets should you enter immediately?

Portfolio of Solutions Profitability

When your product, service, or solution has annuity, it can then yield and be measured for its own profit contribution. If you have several products in your portfolio of solutions—training programs, assessment tools and so on—each will yield its own profit margin. You can then apply an ROI formula to each one.

Average consultants often tend to fall in love with particular solutions. This can be a significant factor in keeping them in the mediocre performance category. It is important to note that many consultants at Levels 1 and 2 may have established solution–annuity relationships with clients; for example, regular purchases of assessment tools for the HR department. A thorough assessment of the profitability contribution of each of your solutions can help free you up to join the top 5% to 10% of consultant earners.

A consultant commented, "I didn't raise the prices of the assessment tools I provide for three years. Now I have to condition my client for sticker shock this year. This is going to take a lot of my time because the organization requires three sign-offs. In retrospect I might have built in a cost escalator into the first agreement. I also need to find support; we have a high volume of assessment orders which is taking away from my valuable time."

Remember, your most valuable asset is your time plus your expertise (merged to become your earning capacity), so be sure to include the costs of your own time in supporting and administering your portfolio of solutions, including the cost of developing new solutions.

- Which of your services are low profit generators?
- How are you managing solution annuity relationships to minimize your time commitment?
- How can you double or triple your charge-out rates for your premium solutions?
- How are you evaluating new solutions?

Niche Market Profitability

Niche marketing for the Odyssey Consultant allows you to identify and work with your Ideal Clients more easily and more often. Some markets just do not fit, or will not pay the kind of fees you need to reach the top echelons of consulting.

One of the major reasons average consultants stay average is because they work in the wrong markets, where it is difficult for a small consulting firm to maximize its positioning and to charge the value-based fees it deserves.

As you change your psychological paradigm, examine your most and least profitable markets more closely. Are they profitable? Are they fun? Are they both profitable and fun? Keep the sunk cost fallacy in mind. Just because you have already put resources into an area where they cannot yield a good return, that should not stop you from changing your methodologies and diverting your efforts to areas where the potential return is greater.

- Are there markets that you could nurture within a stone's throw of your home or office?
- Are you clinging to markets that no longer yield high returns?

It may be helpful to engage a marketing expert to assist in the research and segmentation of market opportunities. For example, one consultant recognised that new CEOs are acutely aware of the need for executive bench strength to execute strategic initiatives. He therefore commissioned research to discover all new CEO appointments to companies in the $25 million category to offer leadership development and coaching services to those CEOs.

Setting Client Fees and Value Billing

Why is it that one consultant can generate fees of $95,000 per annum, another can generate $250,000, another $500,000, and yet another $1 million plus? Breaking out of old ways of thinking and conventional ways of doing business is the key.

There are two steps in moving into the top echelons of consulting. First, you need to make the decision to become totally committed to achieving this objective. Second, ask yourself the basic question, Has anybody ever done this before? If the answer is yes, then you must learn how they did it and copy the principles and best practices they have used, adding your own nuances. That process is a Level 3 Trusted Advisor leap; it is the grand paradigm shift that captures the essence of the Odyssey process. The long list of consultants who have gone through the Odyssey process and applied these principles to their lives, and their businesses are living proof that this process works.

Your primary objective with regard to fees is to achieve value-based billing compiled on the worth of the talent you deliver.

The core challenge at this juncture centers on your ability to demonstrate to your client that the higher fees you charge are a drop in the ocean compared with the value-added results you can bring. Your overarching objective is to show that your consulting contribution will make or save five, ten, or twenty times your cost to the client. Bringing clarity and meaning to the implication and outcome of a successful execution and implementation is where the full Odyssey process converges. Truly, it is hand, head, heart, and soul consulting. Nowhere does consulting embody the spirit of entrepreneurship and service more than at this point.

To stand firm on your fees, it is important to know the worth of the talent that you deliver. When you say, "My fees are easily justified," you have to know what "easily justified" looks like, and you do this by focusing on the metrics questions throughout the M1 conversation as well as in any further interactions with the client. We will look at this issue more closely when we discuss the talent-driven consulting model.

"Back from the result" thinking involves bringing absolute clarity and focus to the outcome that you will deliver to the client as a result of your talent. The test of how well you have done comes when you discuss fees. If the client says, "I can get it cheaper," then you have done your job badly. Following the Odyssey Arrow process builds incremental value in the mind of the client and offsets the client's bargaining chip of "getting it cheaper."

The correct application of the Odyssey Arrow eliminates fee negotiations further along the process, while allowing you ample opportunity to demonstrate talent and define value.

It seems counterintuitive, but when you do not charge enough, people tend not to believe you. Imagine going to two heart surgeons for the most important operation of your life. The first says that he will do the job for $100. The second surgeon says it will cost $5,000.

Would you risk open-heart surgery for $100? Would you be suspicious about the credentials of this surgeon? Credibility comes from the Latin word *credo*, which means to believe. What you will find is that when the price is higher, the client will tend not to negotiate. In fact, the number one reason consultants lose business is that they do not believe in their own numbers and abilities, and they betray this lack of conviction to the client.

When you buy something cheap, you tend to treat it with less respect. When you invest a large amount of money on something, its perceived value grows exponentially, and you treat it with great care and respect.

A second point: Suppose by working through the metrics of a project you have demonstrated to your client that it will save them $500,000. The client then asks, "How much are you going to charge for this?"

If you respond by saying "$800 per day," you have immediately weakened your credibility by breaking the link between your talent and its value to the client. By relating your fee directly to your value to the client, you are creating an unassailable argument in your favor.

Consider this story. A machine in a factory produces $250,000 of goods every day. Then one day, the machine breaks down. The factory owner calls in the supervisors, the mechanics, and the engineers, but nobody can set it working again. Then they call Joe, an external consultant, a Master Practitioner in the area.

Joe comes in, asks many pertinent questions, and examines the machine meticulously. Finally, he takes a piece of chalk from his pocket, goes over to a pipe, and makes a mark. He calls down the engineer and says, "Drill here."

They drill there, let out some air, then seal the pipe back up and hit the start button. The machine starts working again, perfectly.

The factory owner is delighted. "Thank you, Joe, now what is your fee?"

"Fifty thousand dollars," Joe replies, and the factory owner says, "Joe, you've only been here for half an hour, that's a mighty large fee!"

"Yes," says Joe. "It's $1 for the chalk and $49,999 to know where to put the chalk mark."

Joe's value is based not on the time he spent fixing the problem but on the value that he contributed to the organization. When this is pointed out to the factory owner, he does not hesitate. The bill is paid, and the owner saves $200,000 with Joe's intervention.

Four Basic Categories of Fee Setting

Time

I was reviewing a proposal with a colleague recently. It looked great. It was really well put together and focused on diagnosis and collaboration with the client to identify solutions. However, at the end, it had the following statement: "This project will require 20 days at $800 per day."

My heart sank. In charging $16,000, he was leaving about $40,000 on the table. Charging an hourly or a daily rate for short-term assignments is the standard course of action in the business. This is not what Odyssey consultants do. Do not follow the crowd. Be different.

Fixed Fee

Clients rightly fear the time-based approach to fee setting, particularly for longer-term assignments because of the risk that they will remain open ended, leading to spiraling costs. In a fixed fee arrangement of course, the risk is wholly transferred to you, the consultant. With an Odyssey mind-set, you will ensure that the fixed fee is in line with your talent and the value you deliver.

Retainer

In this model, you agree on a retainer fee and remain on call to the client throughout the contracted period. This kind of arrangement can work out very well, depending on the nature of the relationship and the form of client engagement. It is important to define client expectations, your deliverables, and the scope of work included in the retainer agreement.

Contingency Fees

These fall into the "no results, no fee" category. They are unprofessional and should never be considered by an Odyssey consultant. Imagine suggesting to your doctor that you will pay him if the prescription works out. You should always get paid for the services you render and the value you deliver.

The Odyssey consultant leverages two kinds of inventory: time and expertise. The primary reason the majority of consultants undercharge is that they fail to relate their fees to the quantifiable value proposition they represent to the client. Their focus is too much on time and on activities rather than on the value provided to the client.

Results-Based Consulting

Results-based consulting is a systems-thinking approach in managing the critical first part of the Odyssey process: creating the right kind of relationship with the right kind of client. Results-based consulting has three overlapping elements, as outlined in the three circle model in Figure 5.2.

The degree to which you balance these three essentials will go a long way in determining your success as an Odyssey consultant. Let's look at each in turn.

The Economic Buyer

Returning again to my colleague who had submitted the time-based proposal, I asked him who was his point of contact in the client organization. He told me he was dealing with the senior vice president.

I asked, "Well, who's making the decision with respect to this project?"
"The board," he said.

Figure 5.2   The three essentials of results-based consulting.

Straightaway, we can see that he was disconnected from the economic buyer and that he would have to network to the board if he wanted to see his project go ahead. It is always vital to determine whose agenda positions the fees within the client organization. Although my colleague had done some of the work here, he had jumped the gun and stated his numbers before he had really put the value proposition in place. He had presented a time-based rather than a value-based proposal to someone who could not make a decision on it.

A key question here is, was he forming a professional consultant relationship? My view is that he had not taken enough time to build that relationship with the senior vice president so that he could bring this project to the board, position it with them, and perhaps even make the vice president look like the hero in the process.

Finding the right buyer in the client organization is the absolute prerequisite for a results-based assignment to take place, and the right buyer is the economic buyer.

This means that you must clarify—in your own mind—your value proposition to the client in outcome terms, not in terms of what you do. This means understanding that only certain people will appreciate your offering and the talent that comes with it. To find a decision maker, you must be a decision maker. Make a decision to get to the right person in every client organization. This, you will find, is a learned competency once the decision is made to do so.

The Consultative Relationship

How you conceptually and strategically contract with the ultimate buyer, who is your Ideal Client, is essential. When you are with senior decision makers, always move the discussion to the picture in their head, not the need or solution that you have. When you talk about macro objectives and outcomes, you create the environment to have that conceptual connection. From early on in your relationship, you must discuss, debate, and ask probing questions. This kind of dialogue, where you set out to understand how and what they are thinking, forms the foundation for the relationship of trust and peer level respect from which everything else flows.

The Value/Fees Proposition

Odyssey consultants do not talk about commodity-based solutions; they talk about creating value added through profit and performance improvement.

Clarifying the value in achieving macro objectives keeps the discussion away from fees and leads you ultimately to the position where you deliver value vastly in excess of any fee you might charge.

Keep in mind that most organizations are full of waste. Quality gurus estimate that as much as 30% of company revenue generation is wasted. In other words, if a company is generating revenue of more than $20 million, the waste associated with that activity could be as high as $6 million. Making a saving of just $1 million on this figure goes straight to the bottom line.

Making Your Talent Work for You

Value-based consulting is about putting a value on your work and your talent. If you position yourself as a profit improvement specialist, that is, a Level 3 or 4 player, rather than somebody who brings generic solutions to the table, you give your client clear reasons for proceeding with you. Moreover, reasons are more powerful than the features or benefits of any methodology you may have.

When you can demonstrate that your solution is an investment rather than a cold cost, and one with a high return at that, resistance is lowered, and it is easier to move forward. Remember too that most other consultants do not operate in this way. The best Odyssey deals will be larger and have no competitors at the table.

Managers and consultants alike are frequently confused about the term "adding value." In a small assignment, "value" means that your product or service will meet the client's requirements at a fair price. Adding value therefore is exceeding the client's requirements. In the consulting world, there are all sorts of opportunities to add value to your offering, such as the following:

- Being the expert on call for six months after the assignment is completed
- Conducting a teleconference to reinvigorate or challenge the client team
- Sending an e-zine or a valuable e-mail
- Being a sounding board for a client over lunch
- Doing your own mystery shopping research and providing feedback

Although these examples may help to exceed client expectations, they are operational value additives and should not be confused with the big question of need in the mind of the economic buyer or the key value proposition that you represent.

Levels 3 and 4 economic buyers see value as ROI and wealth creation. To help the client improve the bottom line, you must talk about financial performance, profit drivers, and the big picture. In a major assignment, it is imperative that you talk savings, costs, ROI, and metrics.

In his book *Good to Great* (2001), Jim Collins points out how important it is to identify the correct "economic denominator." This is the critical number that determines the ongoing success or failure of a business. In a mainstream business, a top manager will have three or four critical numbers in their head all the time. Your engagement must relate to the client's key numbers, and your dialogue must then be linked to an investment proposition to achieve these targets.

If you are dealing with functional Level 2 managers on a major contract, it is important that you help them position and sell the proposition upstairs. Middle-range functional managers may be good at selling operational performance to their boss but may not have the skills to sell financial ROI performance. This is why you must work shoulder to shoulder with them if your proposition is one that has to be signed off at CEO or board level.

Making the Client a Hero

I had worked for quite some time with the HR manager in a retail company. She was happy with the work I had done and was very comfortable in the relationship. So, I had what I call "the leveraging conversation." I knew that the company had done some strategic planning, so I asked her if there was anything coming out of that process that was going to challenge her as the HR manager. She talked at length about an onboarding process that was in the pipeline and the challenges it would create within the ranks. Although she had done some work on it, she really needed help to bring it to the next level.

She told me, "I'd like to see the CEO take this on, but I'm not really that good at influencing those guys ..."

I suggested we both make a presentation to the CEO. She loved the idea. In the weeks that followed, I spent a lot of time coaching her on the presentation, and when it came time to face the CEO, I put her front and center. It went really well. The CEO said, "I really like what you're doing here. You need to come back to me with a full-blown plan."

He eventually commissioned a $70,000 project, although it ended up closer to $100,000 with additional consulting elements.

Things do not always work out quite as well as they did in this scenario. It really helped that the HR manager in question was highly motivated and saw herself as occupying a strategic role in the organization. If you are dealing with a function head who does not see beyond their own bailiwick and is in effect just an administrator, that approach will not always bear fruit.

On another occasion, one of our Odyssey consultants was working with the vice president of HR in a client organization and secured a $150,000 leadership development program. This was to be a pilot, leading to a corporate rollout, which would be worth an additional $1 million. The consultant *assumed* that senior management was being kept abreast of the program, but this turned out not to be the case. The pilot was rolled out and deemed successful within HR. However, the consultant was shocked when the full corporate program was mothballed. It turned out that the CEO and the COO felt that the program would be disruptive to the culture of the organization. Despite assurances from the vice president of HR that all was well, neither the CEO nor the COO had been part of the early discussion on the program model and methodology.

Keep in mind that in a major assignment, there may be multiple influencers, some of whom will be behind your project and others who will play politics and do everything in their power to sabotage the intervention. Each of these people must be identified, their actions analyzed, and a strategy to win them over devised and put in place. This could take months, even years. Keep asking yourself, who are the key players? Who has the respect of top management?

Sometimes, it is not possible to meet the ultimate decision maker, the economic buyer in the first instance. Working with buyers who have different roles is part and parcel of a major, complex consulting case. If circumstances dictate, you can gather information from the owner of the problem, functional managers, and even user–buyers, long before you get the opportunity to meet the CEO and the board.

There are of course exceptions to every rule, but you will be dealing with and selling into teams nine out of ten times. Every CEO and economic buyer has a support system around, below, and often above them. They rely on these people to help them steer the business. Remember too that influence tends to be less visible than authority; sometimes the people with influence on the back channels of the organization have a great deal more personal and positional power than the formal organizational structure might suggest.

- Who are the key people who influence the influencers?
- How will you empower your champion?
- What is the informal organization structure?
- Who is the real owner of this assignment?
- Who has the real clout in the organization?

Opportunities Abound

Sometimes, when consultants are struggling, they may blame external factors such as the marketplace or clients. They get stuck in a negative spiral of emotions, which is not healthy for the consultant's self-esteem or their business. Self-mastery and shifting focus positively is critical to managing self, brand, expertise, and talent.

You have met the enemy. It is you.

Do not be discouraged. Remember, value is in the eye of the beholder. Opportunities are everywhere. You need not go a long distance to find opportunity. More than any other factor, your unique selling proposition determines your engagement and fee. Consider the following questions:

- What is your unique proposition?
- What is your area of expertise?
- Define your value contribution.
- How congruent are your branding and marketing strategies?

Great consultants—Odyssey consultants—focus on ideas, concepts, models, strategy, value creation, and outcomes. The vast majority of average consultants focus on deliverables, events, needs, and time. They scratch their heads and wonder about the nonperformance of their businesses. Running a low-profit consulting practice, with non-Ideal Clients, is a vicious circle. It is the "peddler syndrome" that takes you out of the professional business category.

Remember, no business is often better than poor business. Remember also that bad business could have been good business that you accepted at the wrong price because you were poorly positioned.

To restate, set your fees based on the value provided, not the time spent or what you do. Be absolutely clear about the 10% to 20% value differentiation that you bring to the assignment. If you do not have that 10% to 20%

difference, then get working on an Odyssey strategy to create your unique-ness in the mind of your client.

The Art and Science of Setting Fees in a Consulting Practice

Setting fees in a professional services business is fundamentally different than price setting in a product-based world. Professional advisors and consultants get paid for services rendered. Their fees reflect not what they do in a particular transaction but rather what they have done over a lifetime of building expertise and experience. They get paid for their talent rather than the product they deliver. You cannot easily price talent, whereas there are many time-honored formulae for pricing a product.

There is a story told about Picasso. He was sitting outside a café in Paris when along came a father and son. The father recognized the great artist and approached him.

"Mr. Picasso, would you be so kind as to do a little sketch for my six-year-old son?"

"Yes indeed," said Picasso, who took out a paper napkin and completed a short sketch, then and there.

"Oh thank you, Mr. Picasso!" said the man. "Such a privilege! Such an honour! Let me give you a donation."

Picasso said, "No, no, no," and the man said, "Oh, I insist. I insist."

Picasso shrugged and said, "Okay, one million francs."

The man stood back and gasped. "But Mr. Picasso, all it took you was five minutes!"

"Oh, but that's where you're wrong my friend," said Picasso. "It didn't take me five minutes to do this. It took me my whole lifetime."

As an Odyssey consultant, you must make the paradigm shift from a product-based, commodified view of the world to one where your talent and intellectual gallantry is rewarded for the real value contribution you make in meeting the challenge that the client presents.

In the product-based world, your competitors and customers go a long way in determining the price of your product. In value-based consulting, you are not in a race with your competitors. You are in a race of one, where you differentiate your talent and intelligence to such a degree that the value-based fees you charge are actually welcome.

Charging appropriate fees is directly related to the caliber and quality of the relationship you have developed with the client. Your courage and clarity are vital in justifying the value-added proposition. Again, value is in the eye of the beholder (Figure 5.3).

This graphic captures the two ways of looking at metrics and how they relate to fees. The upper section illustrates the fee dynamics of talent-driven consulting, and the lower shows the dynamics of time-driven, activity-orientated consulting. If you are simply charging for what you deliver today—the workshop, the survey, the coaching, whatever it is—you are living in the lower part of the model. On the upper half, you are charging for achieving results. You are looking at the value added you achieve by bringing higher sales, profit improvement, reduced costs, and strategic advantage to the client.

By going south, you are looking at time and inputs and task-driven consulting. By going north, you are looking at talent-driven consulting that focuses on outputs, ROI, and value-driven results and outputs.

Based on the Objectives of the Client as You Both Diagnose It

Talent-Driven Consulting

Focus on Outputs / ROI / Value

(Higher Sales; Profit Improvement;
Reduced Costs; Strategic Advantage)

Are You Charging for Added Value Results You Achieve?

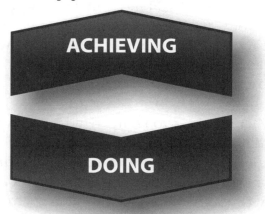

ACHIEVING

DOING

Are You Charging for the Work You Deliver?

(Day; Workshop; Survey; 360; Coaching, i.e., "deliverables")

Focus on Inputs / Time / Task

Time-Driven Consulting

Based on the Needs of the Client as They See It

Figure 5.3   Talent-driven consulting.

Time-based consulting is founded on the needs of the client as they alone see it. They call you in to do a survey, a workshop, or an assessment where you are paid on a piece-work basis (Levels 1 and 2). With talent-driven consulting, you and the client collaborate and partner to diagnose and cocreate custom high-value, long-term solutions (Levels 3 and 4).

If you want to move into the higher echelons of the profession and become a talent-driven consultant, what action steps must you take?

- What do you need to stop doing?
- What might you need to start doing?
- What might you need to continue doing?

The Client/Consultant Value Match

Talent-driven consulting is about building primary relationships with your client, which may be a single person or an entire organization. In either case, the most important objective is to ensure that the relationship with the organization is nurtured through your champion and advocate, who has the power to invite you in at the right level to meet the right people at the right time and place.

Building that relationship takes time. Consultants, driven by their impatience, misplaced instinct to commodity sell and urgent revenue hunger, often miss this most important lesson. It is about several strategic meetings, networking, mapping out staged agendas, mini presentations, and generally taking the longer view ... and following the Odyssey Arrow.

Begin by profiling your current client base. Are you connecting with the right buyer to deliver a value-based service? Your relationship, which must be one of peer-level respect, is best served by connecting with the key stakeholders in the organization, which include the economic buyer, the technical buyer, and the user buyer, as well as the all-important advocate and champion.

Examine your current clients to achieve an intimate appreciation and understanding of their business:

- The psychographics and the demographics
- Business model, vision, strategy
- Size, shape, structure, metrics, industry sector
- Culture and modus operandi
- Stage of growth and development

Presence Creates Value

During the marketing and branding module of the Odyssey Competent Consultant program, a consultant commented on the promotion of his practice. He said, "Promotion is a key ingredient of my marketing strategy. I have used advertising and social media extensively to provide an array of promotional opportunities."

As our coaching sessions progressed, he began to realize that this was not the solution for developing his consulting practice.

The business of consulting is different from other businesses. It demands a more personalized and sophisticated promotional strategy. Average consultants do not understand this concept. They tend to copy traditional promotional methodologies and eventually discover that these methods are both expensive and ineffective.

The promotion of your consulting practice must be centered around you and your principal consultant presence (PCP): your personality, style, skills, values, emotional intelligence—in short—your unique factors, together with your portfolio of solutions. For *who you are* and *what you do* are inextricably linked in consulting. The client contracts you first, then what you do.

This is not to say that the Internet's wide array of promotional opportunities cannot help, but blogging regularly and maintaining high visibility online cannot be seen as a substitute for the previously mentioned factors.

Consider how much time and money you are spending right now on promotion. Are you getting a sufficient return on this investment?

- Packaging *you* is the vital promotional element of your sales and marketing strategy. First impressions really count in consulting. Critically assess your visual appeal and image. Are you dressed for success?
- How professional do your presentation materials and portfolio of solutions appear? Are they congruent with who you are?
- Consult a designer who understands your personality, business model, and portfolio of solutions, one whose concepts will radiate professionalism, excellence, and, of course, *you*!

The consultant in the Odyssey Competent Consultant program who realized that he had been misdirecting his promotional strategy ended up starting afresh. He dumped his website and instead built out his "presence," defining who he was and what he did as a consultant. The result was a confident, talented individual, being the consultant he wanted to be and doing the work he loved doing.

Remember, your reputation and track record represent intangible yet hard-earned and vital assets in consulting. Creating a reputation for uniqueness, difference, and high-value results is a springboard for charging value-based fees, for rendering the intangible tangible, and contributing to presence and profit. A powerful PCP and a sterling reputation deliver powerful value.

The Consultant as an Investor

Consulting, as we have seen, has the potential to generate very significant revenues. In that context, it is possible to identify four discreet levels of financial positioning through which a successful consultant moves as their career progresses (Figure 5.4).

At the first level, as an employee, you have limited control over your cash flow. You take your pay every two weeks or every month as is customary and seek bonuses or raises to try to supplement that cash flow. Your tax position is largely a given; you pay at high marginal levels with little scope for improvement.

As you move into self-employment, you have greater opportunity to drive cash flow into your business. You have the autonomy to seek opportunity and ascend the pyramid to become the business owner, where, once again, your potential to source opportunity and additional cash flow is further enhanced.

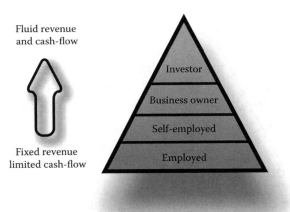

Figure 5.4   Investor pyramid.

As you progress towards the top of the pyramid and become a consultant investor, you can take the profits you have generated through your experience and expertise and invest them in the stock market, in real estate, or other businesses and, thereby, develop a passive income to complement your earnings as a consultant. The central objective here is to become the investor: The money works for you! You harness the cash flow in your business to make third-party investments, which deliver an investment income while you engage your passion in the consulting business.

The Value of the Generalist and the Specialist

Clients today want every consultant to have the generalist skills of their best general manager and at the same time the in-depth knowledge of a technical specialist. This presents a dilemma to the Odyssey consultant. On the one hand, the more specialized your approach, the smaller the market you will have available to you. On the other hand, the more generalist you are, the less credible you might appear in the eyes of the client. The following sections present the four approaches you can take to help bridge this gap.

Specialize

We live in a society that produces and prefers specialists. Overspecializing in consulting, however, will buy you a ticket on the feast and famine roller coaster. Moreover, the business world is changing so rapidly that even maintaining your particular specialization is frequently a challenge. How do you deal with expectations from clients? As an Odyssey consultant, go with the notion that you are a specialist. Create your business model and messaging in a way that your one-person practice specializes in whatever the client requirement is. Your specialty might be human resources, but if you also develop managerial skills, you can bring in and coordinate the overall intervention, contracting resources from other specialists (technology, finance, etc.) as necessary.

Be Clear about Your Difference

Your area of excellence is your competitive advantage. Differentiate yourself as an Odyssey consultant by maintaining the uniqueness of your portfolio of solutions and personal branding. Think about the perceptions you wish to create, about how you will leave a lasting impression in your client's mind.

Demonstrate through your marketing and promotion your differentiators, presence, and consistency.

Who you are, your character and personality, your look, what you do, and how you do it when you are on site with the client separate the amateur from the professional in the field of consulting.

Define Your Ideal Clients

Segmentation is the act of systematically identifying your Ideal Client mix. Resist the temptation to market your portfolio of solutions to everyone, everywhere. Some consultants like travelling long journeys by air and by car to meet their clients. The reality is that if you are spending time collecting air miles, you are not spending time finding or serving clients. Yes, it is a global village and international assignments are exciting, but it is a matter of doing a thorough cost–benefit analysis and deciding whether the assignment is actually worth it or whether it is just an expensive ego trip.

It often makes more sense to operate locally, to target and handpick clients who value what you do and are prepared to pay the consulting fees that you deserve for the value that you create.

Any business is better than no business is an old maxim. This is self-limiting thinking. Learn to say no. Your motto must be "the right business, the right client, the right revenue." Your time and talent deserve better. You can be just as busy generating total fees of $200,000 as generating fees of $1 million.

Focus, Focus, Focus

Your ability to focus and concentrate all of your marketing, promotion, and intellectual efforts on building relationships with your Ideal Clients is the essence of Odyssey consulting. Expending time and effort in the wrong market segments with low-value clients imposes a ceiling on your potential to grow and develop your consulting practice. Be crystal clear and totally focused in your thinking and actions:

- What is your purpose?
- What are you really good at?
- What do you love to do?
- What is your key talent?
- What are your core competencies?
- What is your value-driven proposition?

Odyssey in Action I

Mark Debinski, Bluewater Advisory & Bluewater Search, Sykesville, Maryland

Before You Do the Business, You've Got to Find It

The reason I'm such a staunch supporter of the planning and budgeting process is that I've seen so often what can happen when you don't do it. When I first started consulting, I had two partners: myself, a legacy senior consultant that had been around for a long time, and one other guy—Bob—who had been a banker for twenty years.

We put a fee share arrangement in place. You "eat what you kill." When you sold work, a portion went to the house for overhead and marketing, and the rest was yours.

Bob he was on board with everything verbally. Then, at the end of the first month he got a check for $2,000.

He was shocked. "Two thousand dollars? I can't live on two thousand dollars. I've got kids getting ready for college!"

"Bob," I said, "what were you thinking?"

It quickly emerged that he had never fully processed the fact that you need to sell work and then do the work and then get paid for the work. There was never going to be an automatic paycheck that would show up on time and for the right amount every second week.

One of the things I've found with many consultants I've met is that while they may have the competencies while they may understand the "knowledge transfer" piece the "actual running a business" piece? That's lacking.

I have people contacting me on a weekly basis, telling me that they've decided to become a consultant. Often, I get the impression that they think they're doing me a favor because they want to join my team.

Typically, I say, "Well I'm flattered. Tell me how much business are you bringing with you and how much business do you plan to do in the first year?"

Then there's a pregnant pause, followed by something like, "Oh, well, I know that you're really busy and I just figured and I would come and work with your clients …"

There's a real misconception by many consultants about the rainmaking portion of the business development: pricing it properly, closing the deal, then seeing it through a conclusion.

First off, you need to develop a plan around where you're going to get business. You need to understand the sell cycle. I might have an initial meeting with a prospect, but it could be two months, three months, or six months after that conversation before that client is ready to fully engage. You work on their time frame, not yours.

I have a friend that's starting a consultancy right now, and I've given him all of my budgeting and planning tools, but he hasn't used them. Instead, he's filling his calendar with coffee meetings, breakfast meetings, dinner meetings, and all of that. I call it the shotgun approach and it won't work. He hasn't developed a strategy around where the low-hanging fruit is, where he's going to get the business.

When I started out, I didn't have the luxury of being able to fail. I had worked in various organizations for twenty years, but it had always been my plan to become a consultant. From the very beginning, I wanted to be my own boss. I wanted to make a lot of money, and I wanted to have the freedom to do things like go to my girls' track meets. I wanted to have the opportunity for high income and freedom, freedom of the wheres and the whens. That doesn't mean that I don't work crazy hours—I do—but I find the harmony in the flexibility that comes with being a consultant.

I'm the sole earner in our household. We have a fairly expensive lifestyle simply because of schools and elder care and all those things that go with raising a family. For me, the consequences of failure would have been very, very serious.

And so it wasn't a question of "Can I make a good deal of money?" It was this: "If I'm going to do this, I have to make a good deal of money."

I had been in business for two years before I went through Odyssey. Afterwards, my revenues increased five- or sixfold.

What Odyssey did was it helped me get clarity around what I was good at, what areas of consulting I enjoyed, and where I could make the most money. It showed me how to work—in Odyssey parlance—at Levels 3 and 4, how to find the right prospects, and how to create a strategy for getting in front of them.

Odyssey in Action II

Vicki Lauter, Managing Partner, Strategic Human Insights, Atlanta, Georgia

The Test Comes When You Quote Your Price

When I started back in 2001, my business was retained executive search for the healthcare industry. I had worked in that area in Accenture, and in Ernst and Young before that. And when I started out, it was great. I made a lot of money, I loved my clients, and I loved what I was doing.

In the US, people were having a hard time finding the right candidates for the right roles. But what started happening with me is that I ended up giving away a lot of services for free. You don't know what you don't know, right? There was so much I didn't know about building a business, about the financial side. I just loved what I was doing, and I wanted to help people as much as possible.

The thing is, you're providing a huge amount of value. They know it, so they're taking advantage of you in a sense because you're not smart enough to recognize that you should really change your pricing. For some clients, I was basically doing the HR job and not getting paid for it.

So I went to Odyssey in 2011. The program helped me to realize that I was providing more value than I was being paid for. We know that all business is not good business, and while it's not fun to lose a client, you can't waste your time on somebody that doesn't really get your value, some-one who's thinking, "I'm getting a whole lot and she's not smart enough to know to charge me more ..."

I always remember John Butler in the marketing webinar saying, "When you quote your price, the test is going to come." I thought that was interest-ing at the time, but I didn't really understand it until I came home and actu-ally put it to the test.

After Odyssey, I got my ducks together. I had the fee conversation, the one John set so much store by, with two different companies. Was it uncom-fortable? Yes, it was. I got sick to my stomach. But the one thing that I real-ized, and the one thing that continues to hold true today is this: I know that I provide tremendous value to my Ideal Clients.

One client just didn't get it. I told them that I could no longer work with them as I had in the past. But they didn't want to pay the money, so I said, "Well that's okay," and I walked away.

The other client was a consulting firm in the healthcare sector. The proj-ect involved taking their recruiting process and completely reorganizing it. At first, they balked at the fee. They were like, "Wow. Really? That seems to be a lot of money."

I just said, "Well ... no. At the end of the year, you'll see whether or not this makes financial sense, and if it doesn't, I'll give you your money back."

They had been in a massive, ongoing struggle to find and retain the right people. But by the end of the project, their turnover rate was down to 10%.

For the consulting industry—where the turnover rate frequently hits 50%—this was a real result.

At the end of the year, we were able to show them how their retention figures had changed as a result of our work. They said, "Yeah we knew that things were going a lot smoother and we were getting a lot more people hired. We didn't realize how well it was going until we actually stopped and really focused on it."

I was able to demonstrate that we had saved them $54,800. My fee for was $12,500. As John Butler used to say, "It was a drop in the bucket."

Chapter Summary

In this chapter, we examined the six profit drivers collectively responsible for the success of a consulting business. We looked at how Odyssey consultants differentiate themselves by setting fees based on talent rather than the time spent on a consulting assignment, and we outlined the art and science of fee setting and the four basic fee setting options.

We then introduced the three essential components of results-based consulting: the economic buyer, the consultative relationship, and the value/fees proposition. Value-based consulting continued this theme by examining the metrics on which the Odyssey consultant must remain focused when laying the groundwork for Levels 3 and 4 client relationships. We then looked at how talent-driven consulting differs from time-driven, activity-orientated consulting. Promoting your practice as an Odyssey consultant requires a more sophisticated and personalized PCP approach. Finally, we examined the value of being a hybrid of specialist and generalist consultant in driving your business growth.

Calls to Action

1. Assess your profit drivers. Identify your strong and weak links. What corrective measures will you take?

   _____

   _____

   _____

   _____

_____

_____

_____

2. How do you currently set client fees. How will you integrate a value-based billing strategy into your client assignments?

_____

_____

_____

_____

_____

_____

_____

_____

3. How comfortable are you in connecting appropriately with key decision makers and understanding their metrics? Describe how you will raise your comfort level.

_____

_____

_____

_____

_____

_____

_____

4. What market segment(s) does your practice favor? How do you differentiate your expertise and your practice methodology? Be specific.

_____

_____

_____

_____

_____

_____

_____

5. Think about your current principal consultant presence (PCP). Define the changes you could make to make it more powerful.

_____

_____

_____

_____

_____

_____

_____

_____

_____

Bibliography

Collins, J. (2001). *Good to Great*. New York: HarperCollins.

Collins, J. (2002). *Built to Last*. New York: HarperCollins.

Coyle, D. (2013). *The Green Platform*. Bray, Ireland: Ballpoint Press.

Hedges, K. (2011). *The Power of Presence: Unlock Your Potential to Influence and Engage Others*. New York: AMACON Publishing.

Heweltt, S. A. (2014). *Executive Presence: The Missing Link between Merit and Success*. New York: HarperCollins.

Malloy, J. T. (1996). *New Women's Dress for Success*. New York: Hatchet Book Group.

Malloy, J. T. (2008). *New Dress for Success*. New York: Hatchet Book Group.

McChesney, C., Covey, S., & Huling, J. (2012). *The 4 Disciples of Execution*. New York: Simon & Schuster.

Weiss, A. (2002). *Value-Based Fees: How to Charge—and Get—What You're Worth*. San Francisco: Jossey-Bass/Pfeiffer.

Chapter 6

The Mind-Set Factor

- Have you got what it takes to break through your mind-set barriers to success?
- How do you define your consulting success?
- How is your mind-set serving you in life and business?

This chapter examines the Odyssey consultant mind-set, which will always be preeminent to the Odyssey consultant skill set. We look at how you define and measure success as a professional advisor and show how to calibrate your own success in a holistic way. We explore the power of harnessing positive psychology, which is central to cultivating the Odyssey consultant mind-set. Embracing personal responsibility and understanding the wider applications of the responsibility issue provide a foundational discipline for so much of the work that successful consultants do.

Beyond the Mental Game of Consulting

Consulting based on your talent can be subdivided into a range of distinct areas itemized in Figure 6.1. Frequently, the talents that you will harness to become a great consultant are hiding in plain sight and are often taken for granted. They are so interwoven through life/work experience that they can be difficult to unravel and identify. Talent does however leave clues. Take a look at the graphic and consider it in the context of your own life and work.

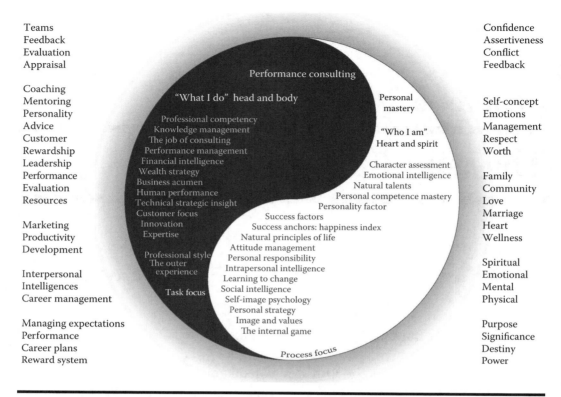

Teams
Feedback
Evaluation
Appraisal

Coaching
Mentoring
Personality
Advice
Customer
Rewardship
Leadership
Performance
Evaluation
Resources

Marketing
Productivity
Development

Interpersonal
Intelligences
Career management

Managing expectations
Performance
Career plans
Reward system

Confidence
Assertiveness
Conflict
Feedback

Self-concept
Emotions
Management
Respect
Worth

Family
Community
Love
Marriage
Heart
Wellness

Spiritual
Emotional
Mental
Physical

Purpose
Significance
Destiny
Power

Performance consulting

"What I do" head and body

Professional competency
Knowledge management
The job of consulting
Performance management
Financial intelligence
Wealth strategy
Business acumen
Human performance
Technical strategic insight
Customer focus
Innovation
Expertise

Professional style
The outer
experience

Task focus

Personal
mastery

"Who I am"
Heart and spirit

Character assessment
Emotional intelligence
Natural talents
Personal competence mastery
Personality factor
Success factors
Success anchors: happiness index
Natural principles of life
Attitude management
Personal responsibility
Intrapersonal intelligence
Learning to change
Social intelligence
Self-image psychology
Personal strategy
Image and values
The internal game

Process focus

Figure 6.1   The consultant's talent management model.

The talent management model encompasses the yin and yang of life. Left of the circle, on the performance consulting side, the focus is on *what* you do and corresponds to the head and hand in the four levels of the consulting model. It is composed of the skills, knowledge, and competencies of the individual, all of which merge to deliver the *task focus* necessary to manage a consulting engagement.

The opposite side of the graphic is all about personal mastery. In terms of the four levels of the consulting model, it focuses on *who* you are. This is the heart and the spirit dimension and embraces deeper personal qualities such as emotional intelligence, personal responsibility, beliefs, and values. These characteristics combine to deliver a *process focus* as distinct from the task focus on the left hand side of the model.

The left-hand column, which sits outside the circle, lists the range of consulting topics that you may engage in as your chosen area. The skill sets listed within the diagram are then applied to whichever niche you have adopted to achieve the task focus required.

The competent consultant will successfully integrate yin and yang to create congruence in their lives and businesses, seamlessly merging who they are on the inside with what they do on the outside.

Converting Your Talents into Strategic Competencies

Competencies are created by the combination of behaviors, attitudes, values, skills, learned practices, and emotional intelligence and are applied by effective people to deliver superior results.

Competencies are also derived from your talents and are manifested through your aptitude and attitude. Your talents are often obvious, yet they may not always convert into the competencies that get superior results. Therefore, a clear understanding of your talents is an essential first step in achieving superior competence and consulting excellence. You are unlikely to reach your full potential unless you are working in harmony with your talents.

The Odyssey Trusted Advisor Competency Model

We in Odyssey have developed a Trusted Advisor competency model. This framework identifies the requirements for superior consulting performance, measures the individual against that benchmark, and sets forth a development plan to enable best results.

The process measures the consultant's talents against the Odyssey consultant benchmark. The gaps identified in the process then become areas for development. As you work on those competencies, you will add value to your practice which will in turn add to your value and influence with clients. This process can also be implemented in a client workplace where job definitions are unclear, and it can also be extended to recruitment and career path development.

Your challenge as an Odyssey consultant is to meet and surpass the talent requirements of the Trusted Advisor and to turn your natural talents into competencies that transform your performance and results.

Defining Success as a Professional Advisor

What is success? How do you define success as a consultant and as a professional services firm? How successful are you as a professional? What criteria do you use to determine how you're doing in your business? What do you need to stop doing or start doing to be more successful in your professional practice?

There are many myths and much confusion about the concept of success. Who motivates the motivator? Sometimes you are so busy directing, managing, helping, mentoring, coaching, and consulting with your clients that you forget to "sharpen the saw" for yourself.

As a consulting professional, success must be universally defined to embrace your full life, not just one or two aspects of it. Many managers and business owners focus solely on the financial returns or results of success while ignoring the antecedents. Conversely, other professionals fall in love with the passion and freedom that their profession provides and sometimes neglect the reality of the business or personal side.

Take a conscious look at how you have defined success in your work and life before consulting and how you are defining it now that you are in consulting. This exercise is very important as it will inform your consulting practice and business priorities. It may be helpful to engage a coach to assist you in discovering fresh insights and to bring clarity and focus to what you already know about your current situation and to plan your future direction. It is also important to expose faulty assumptions about success and what it means for you as a successful consultant within a successful consulting business.

Six Dimensions of Success

Notice how four of the following six dimensions of success start with the phrase "to be" and one each with "to have" and "to do."

1. To be happy and have peace of mind

Peace of mind means being in control of your own destiny ... to enjoy the journey of life and work; to have the right balance and integration between personal and professional life; to feel connected physically, mentally, emotionally and spiritually to both sides of the work life equation; to be carefree; to laugh often; just "to be," less "have" and "do" and more "be."

Happiness is the progressive realization of a worthy goal. You are likely to be happiest when you tune into your heart's desire. What motivates you? Are your goals clear? Do you feel you are creating the opportunity to do your best work? Do you think you are acquiring the opportunity to do enough of your best work to make it financially viable? These questions should prompt you to assess the values at the very core of who you are and how they dovetail with your consulting business.

The key to happiness, both as a person and as a consultant, is your determination to dedicate yourself to a worthwhile purpose by developing mastery in the personal and professional competencies that are consistent with your natural talents, behaviors, values, and intelligence. You cannot be truly happy until you are clear about the inherent possibilities within your own person.

In general, happy people are those with high levels of self-respect, self-esteem, confidence, and personal pride. They have come to appreciate the real value they contribute to their clients and never allow it to be downgraded to a lesser status than it deserves. Lack of self-confidence is the number one inhibitor of exceptional performance. It hurts the client and consultant equally. Odyssey focuses on building consultants' confidence.

Many unhappy people fail to take responsibility for this anchor ingredient of success. You will never achieve peace of mind and happiness by simply "trying to be happy." Rather, it seems to come naturally as a result of doing worthwhile work, where both you and the client collaborate as peers and have clear respect for each other.

Unhappiness is encapsulated in the ugly secret of life, and that secret is *fear*. Fear manifests itself in self-doubt, poor self-image, shyness, guilt, blaming, anxiety, mental distress, and disorder. In the context of a professional practice, these negative emotions can also manifest in an overfocus on deliverables, inputs, timeframes, tasks, and low fee-setting. Aggregated together, these things rob us of peace of mind and our natural right to be happy.

By contrast, confidence and competence go hand in hand with the top echelons of professional work. One will never be found without the other.

The good news is negative emotions can be unlearned. Your current position on the happiness–unhappiness scale is more framed around who you are and the past choices you have made and less around your technical abilities. The bottom line, however, is that you deserve to be happy and have peace of mind.

An excellent way to change your position on the scale is to take total personal responsibility for learning how to redefine and reframe happiness, in both your personal and professional contexts, with life and work integration as the goal.

2. To be in good physical health

Good health means being fit and energetic, to have a sense of vitality and a zest for living. It means eating well, exercising, and resting enough to replenish the body. The reality of course is that it is vitally important to care for your body as well as your mind.

Nature has a natural bias towards balance and harmony. Your body has a natural bias towards health and energy. Only improper treatment can knock it out of balance. Just as your inner voice will tell you if your peace of mind is offtrack, your body will let you know it is out of alignment through lethargy, pain, and illness. It is imperative that you actively manage your physical and mental health needs.

The Alameda Study (2005) was a pioneering research project that tracked the health habits of 8,000 men for twenty years in Alameda County, CA, to determine factors such as longevity, sickness patterns, and why some men were healthier than others. The seven common habits of the healthiest participants were determined to be as follows:

a. Eating at regular times each day
b. Eating lightly, especially fruit, vegetables, and lean source protein
c. No grazing between meals
d. No smoking
e. Moderate alcohol consumption
f. Being well rested, with seven to eight hours of sleep every night
g. Regular exercise, which helps digestion and the overall "feel" factor

All choices have consequences. Every bite of food, each drink, every cigarette, and every overindulgence affects your health. Consultants need minimal health baggage to be on top of their game.

3. To be committed to quality relationships

The third anchor of success is the quality of your relationships. Interpersonal intelligence has been defined as your overall ability to relate well with others and in consulting, to achieve peer-level respect with the right buyer in client companies. Emotional intelligence is defined as your capacity to manage your emotions and feelings to benefit others while sensing, accepting, appreciating, and mediating the emotions and feelings of others. In consulting, emotional intelligence is an absolute prerequisite. The caliber of your one-to-one relationships, above all, is the ultimate test of who you are.

Remember that your technical competence comes second to your ability to connect with the client at an intrinsic level, to establish rapport; people buy *you* first, then your proposition. Consulting is more often than not a transfer of tempered enthusiasm. Marginal consulting assignments are lost, all other things being equal, because the client just did not believe or trust you. The real questions are as follows: How much do you believe in the merits of your own case? How much do you believe in you? How do you feel about yourself?

The quality of both your personal and professional life is largely determined by your ongoing ability to communicate, interact, influence, and negotiate with other people. Most client relationships are functional, that is, time and circumstance related. However, your ability to connect with and maintain long-lasting genuine friendships with the critical few is vital to this success anchor. As clients' circumstances change and as executives move on, the common thread can be the consultant who has a reputation for consistently solving problems and delivering results. Relationship loyalty is the common denominator.

As a top-class advisor, you are a work in progress, ever growing and learning from experience. Your personal character and professional prowess are shaped, more than any other factor, by how you learn to manage the uniqueness of each client situation.

Top class client work brings interpersonal communication to its highest level. Remember, you are unique and complex; your client is unique and complex. Therefore, relationships are unique and complex and provide the arena to test the most fundamental success anchors: Do you communicate your trustworthiness? Do you consistently deliver discernible value? Are you a talented communicator? Can you tell people what you do in thirty seconds or less? Can you illustrate what you do on the back of a napkin?

Following certain time-honored truths or principles certainly helps:

a. Trust is the willingness to be vulnerable to the actions of another person. Trust means, above all, keeping your word and being reliable, consistent, and dependable.
b. Respect primarily means listening attentively, listening with your eyes, listening with your mind. Listening is often a blind spot for advisors, as they often want to talk and tell. It is important to seek feedback on how well you carry out this vital skill.

    Asking well-thought-out questions that engage the client's mind and heart are vital ingredients in generating respect.

c. Openness in the communication process requires a degree of vulnerability, time, helpfulness, attention, and awareness of the different mind-sets that your client brings to every one-to-one interaction.

d. Appreciation is the final principle. When you say "please" and "thank you," when you recognize contribution (e.g., Thank you for sharing your thoughts with me) and ask permission (e.g., May I ask you a question?), you automatically raise your client's self-esteem and increase the bond between you.

4. To do purposeful work

Making a significant contribution—making a difference—is what defines purposeful work to significantly add more value than your cost. How worthwhile do you feel your work is? Does it have a purpose that matches your talents? Is your work a magnificent obsession?

As definitions of success at work have changed over the last few decades, the role of the consultant has found a new significance. In days past, companies offered their employees the appealing prospect of a job for life, i.e., a career. Loyalty and hard work were rewarded with job security and the prospect of climbing the corporate ladder. Today, quality of life issues and personal/professional growth opportunities are more powerful motivators among many executives and employees. More consultants are providing temporary project-based work as companies hold the line on committing to long-term employment.

The magnificent obsession that drives some consultants and executives is the key to their success and often, ironically, their failure. They find themselves devoting the bulk of their time and energy to their business and very little to family or personal life. Sadly, few seem to know how to regain the balance.

It is possible to achieve mastery at work and have a high-quality family life. However, many clients need the help that consultants can provide to achieve their goals. This is valuable and worthwhile work for both the consultant and the client. In fact, for many clients, it is life saving, transformational, and even "priceless." Your challenge is to sell the value of your services in the first instance and then to enjoy the challenge of delivering it in the second.

5. To have financial freedom

Your ability to create personal and business financial advantage in your consulting business is central to your success as an advisor. Money has a bad reputation because many people perceive they do not have enough of it. People often attempt to rationalize the failure to have money. To justify their lack, you will hear them say, "money is the root of all evil" or "money can't buy happiness." Both of these concepts are incomplete. Money is not the root of all evil, although poor money management could be.

For you as a professional advisor, there are two critical questions:

a. Do you want to be wealthy?
b. Do you want to stay in the middle of the pack or join the elite?

Becoming wealthy from the fruits of your professional service firm is a measure of your ability to command high fees with high margins.

Financial freedom is about building lifetime assets. Wealth generation requires a *can do* mind-set and is the result of smart work, perseverance, planning, and, most of all, self-discipline.

Value-based fees and best practice advisory and execution skills are the learnable competencies necessary to hit the top of professional practice in financial terms, but mind-set is the glue that cements it all together.

6. Self-actualization: to be living a full life

The sixth anchor of success is to embrace the idea that life is for living. Success is a journey, not a destination. Today, to live on the outer edges of your potential means you must be a continuous learner— consciously adapting, changing, and growing. Being an expert advisor is being the ultimate learning professional. Avoid the natural tendency to get back into your comfort zone, a retreat that paralyzes the opportunities that come your way. To help others identify their talents and achieve their goals, you must first use your own talents and achieve your own goals. You must self-actualize to explore and develop your personal and professional potential.

Here are things to consider as you contemplate your success mind-set:

a. In your professional journey, put as much effort into who you are as what you do. Take 100% responsibility for developing your competence and confidence levels. You are unlikely to reach your full potential without having both of these working in splendid harmony. Identifying and working with your God-given talents is as near to fulfilment as you are likely to get.

b. Learn how to be a top class advisor by following a proven success system. Being functionally competent to be an advisor is less than half the battle. The key battle involves a mind-set shift.

c. Never do it alone. Surround yourself with people who will challenge your thinking, your feelings, your behaviors, and your practice. The question asked by one of our MasterClass attendees was, "Who consults to the consultant? Who nurtures the nurturer?"

The mind-set and activities that got you to where you are today may have served you well in the past, but ask yourself how these attributes will serve you in the future. No amount of success in your practice will compensate for personal distress. Do not become a prisoner of your business success at the expense of your peace of mind, health, and close personal relationships. Make a decision to be the most competent advisor possible by applying futuristic thinking and continuous learning with a positive mind-set. A wise grandfather once said to his grandson, "Make a concerted effort to keep in touch with the small people, the tall people, the young and old, and the others you love."

Measuring Your Success

The Rubicon "Total Success" concept identifies six metrics of success.

Allotting ten points per factor, how do you score yourself on each one? For a graphic representation, map your scores onto the wheel and join the dots to represent your success pattern (Figures 6.2 and 6.3).

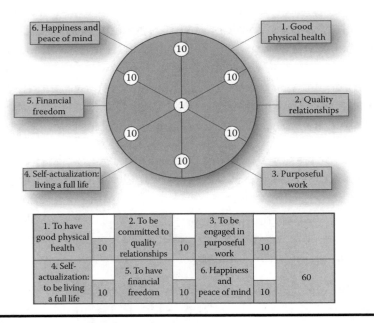

Figure 6.2 The success wheel + scoring grid.

		0	1	2	3	4	5
1	"Success is a journey" How is your journey?						
2	"Success is setting and achieving your definite objectives" Have you clear written objectives?						
3	"To become everything you are capable of becoming" How far along this road are you?						
4	"To thine own self be true" How true to yourself and your talents are you?						
5	"As much as 85% of your success will come from your relationships" What is the caliber of your work and personal relationships?						
6	"Just do it" is the Nike slogan. How action oriented are you, really, on the critical issues?						

Figure 6.3   Success factor grid.

Having determined your success pattern, what action could you take that will enable you to be the best consultant you can be?

The Triple Mind: From Brain Power to Mind Power

Brain power and mind power are not the same. If your brain is your house, your mind is your home. Your brain is structured to be functional; it fulfils much the same function as the hardware in a computer. Innovative research is being conducted on brain power, notably by Dr. Ron Bonnstetter and Dr. Bill Bonnstetter at Target Training International in Phoenix, Arizona.

It is your mind that expands and creates your wisdom and potential, allowing your talents and inherent possibilities to flourish. The mind serves as your software. It is your psychological powerhouse. To understand the mind, it is best described as having three distinct divisions, each with its own separate function:

- The conscious mind
- The subconscious mind
- The superconscious mind

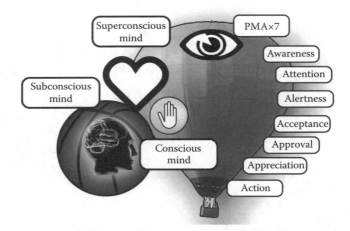

Figure 6.4   Superconsciousness.

The metaphor of the golf ball, the basketball, and the balloon helps to illustrate the size and significance of all three parts of the mind. Your conscious mind (golf ball size) works directly with your brain and is much smaller than the (basketball size) subconscious mind. The superconscious mind (balloon size) is massive compared with the other two but remains underutilized by all but a tiny minority of people (Figure 6.4). Let us explore this important framework in the context of consulting.

The Four Dimensions of the Competent Consultant

The four classic dimensions of the competent consultant emerge almost seamlessly within the triple mind (Figure 6.5):

■ The physical dimension represented by the hand and the five senses is the conscious mind.

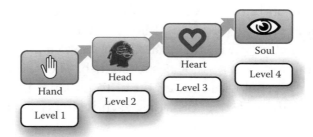

Figure 6.5   The four dimensions of the human being.

- The intellectual dimension represented by the head is the thinking subconscious.
- The emotional dimension represented by the heart straddles the boundary between all three minds, the superconscious.
- The spiritual or soul dimension is represented by the eye because "the eyes are the windows to your soul."

The conscious mind is objective, sensible, discerning, systemic, and extrinsic in how it functions. As your five senses receive data from the thousands of interactions you have with the world every day, the conscious mind clinically analyzes, compares, and decides on a course of action. These are automatic responses in most cases and account for an estimated 10% of your thinking. The conscious mind can only concentrate on relatively few thoughts at a time.

The subconscious mind is your software storage system. Every experience, memory, and influence is stored in your subconscious databank. It reacts to inputs and instructions from the conscious mind. Its programming and retrieval systems, therefore, are only as good as the input. The computer formula "garbage in, garbage out" holds particularly true.

The superconscious mind is concerned with attaining higher and higher levels of consciousness through present moment awareness (PMA). PMA to the power of seven (also called PMA×7) is the process of being hyperconscious, more alert, and more attentive than the normal conscious state.

Full consciousness or super consciousness means being more connected, more centered, more enlightened, and more "in the zone" or "in the now." It is this capacity—for you to be fully present and completely in the now—that separates the amateur consultant from the professional consultant more than any other factor. Pure consciousness is almost a state of "no mind" where you detach or disidentify from the constant chatter—"the monkeys of the mind"—that dominates so many people's thinking.

PMA×7 gives you the option of turning off your own subconscious thinking and tuning into your client and the present moment with more conscious and superconscious awareness. It extends beyond mindfulness and involves the following:

1. Awareness—being fully present and aware of the present moment
2. Attention—to what is being articulated and everything else
3. Alertness—being alert to the total situation and circumstances
4. Acceptance—not judging the person or jumping to solutions

5. Approval—recognizing who they are with unconditional care
6. Appreciation—being empathetic and understanding
7. Action—purposeful action is the way forward; nothing happens without action

Trustworthiness Defined

The trust relationship you develop and build with the client is based on the client's emotional appreciation or disapproval of your presence, skills, and behavior. The client will choose early in the process whether or not to entrust you with their thoughts, feelings, ideas, and problems.

Ten Ways to Create Entrusting Relationships with Your Client

1. Earn the right to offer advice
2. Build incremental candor, professional intimacy, and risk taking
3. Partner rationally (thinking) and emotionally (feeling)
4. Listen actively, intentionally and with PMA, using visual/vocal nudges
5. Use a wide repertoire of questions; use silence effectively
6. Use appropriate humor (avoid sensitive topics)
7. Show your passion for the topic, subject, and role
8. Illustrate and create pictures. Do not talk at or to people
9. Be able to say, assertively, "I don't know"
10. Control and manage your emotions

Ten Ways to Create Distrusting Relationships with Your Client

1. Talking and telling stories about yourself
2. Having all the answers and giving them too quickly
3. Talking more than asking (selfishness)
4. Interrupting the client
5. Needing to be right or intelligent; giving qualifications or name dropping
6. Jumping to conclusions or solutions
7. Ignoring emotional cues and focusing only on rational thinking
8. Depersonalizing the interaction
9. Taking credit for client ideas, solutions
10. Assuming and judging

Positive Psychology—Managing Your Potential and Possibilities

The majority of professional practice firms seek to build positive perspectives for individual clients and client organizations. However, for that to happen, to help the client achieve their purpose, it is imperative that you, the consultant/advisor, set out to achieve your own potential.

Psychology is the science of the natural functions, processes, behaviors, and characteristics of the human mind. Since World War II, much psychology was focused on "what is wrong with people" rather than a "what is right with people." The whole psychology industry had been built around engaging with the downside of human behaviors.

Positive psychology, pioneered by Dr. Martin Seligman and others, has grown more popular over the last decade. It presents a new vision of psychology. The positive psychological perspective looks for the potential in people. It explores how people can flourish and develop their talents rather than simply functioning and letting life pass them by.

Traditional psychology focuses on "specific action tendencies" or why negative emotions (the "fight or flight" response for example) prompt people to act in a certain way. Positive psychology focuses on the effects of positive emotions on behavior patterns. These positive emotions have the potential to change how you think and fuel learning and self-transformation. Personal and professional resources, networks, knowledge, and talents are then broadened to help you manage, grow, and thrive. Positive psychologists call it the "broaden-and-build" theory.

Positive psychology anchors, emotional intelligence, and self-image go hand-in-hand with achieving superior and consistent management competency levels. Positive emotions are vital for consultants in establishing rapport with clients. Research from the Gallup organization shows that client satisfaction (a judgment) does not always translate into high fees, but emotional bonding (a positive feeling) actually creates loyalty and generates increased fees. Being "recognized as a human being" rather than as a transaction is the primary motivation for peer-level respect and loyalty.

For experts in general, the difference between knowing about positive psychology and translating it into one's personal and professional life remains the challenge. The Odyssey consultant embarks on a conscious journey to enhance their positive psychology and tune up the natural talents that contribute to their unique music. One of the great tragedies of life is that most people go to their graves with their music still in them.

Your Self-Concept and How It Affects Your Consulting Practice

Self-concept is made up of your natural inborn talents, nurtured attributes, beliefs, values, emotional intelligence and learned experiences. As a consultant, your performance potential is directly related to your self-concept. It tends to predict your degree of mastery in your area of endeavor.

Your self-concept is stored in your subconscious mind and controls your thoughts, feelings, behaviors, and actions. It triggers your responses to people, situations, and circumstances. Its memory storehouse is huge and tends to categorize every incident as a belief or as a habit, depending on your early life conditioning. You have hundreds of mini self-concepts for all areas of your life, some are good and some are not so good.

Your self-concept is made up of three overlapping parts: self-ideal, self-image, and self-esteem. Understanding how these three elements work together is essential to your overall interpersonal and applied competency, your talent delivery, and long-term success (Figure 6.6).

1. Your self-ideal is the person you would most like to become—"the future me." It helps determine your current strategies, future purpose, and create direction in life. It can act as the motivator for growth and change as a consultant. When people leave the corporate world and choose to be a consultant, the ideal self is a work in progress.

2. Your self-image determines your current performance—"the current me." It is how you view your current self, your presence and capabilities, and how valuable you feel yourself in the moment, as a person and as professional advisor.

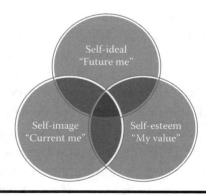

Figure 6.6   The three parts of the self.

3. Your self-esteem is the emotional evaluation of one's own worth. Self-esteem can involve a variety of beliefs about the self and is heavily influenced by your self-ideal and your self-image.

Let us look at each of these in turn.

Your Self-Ideal

Your self-ideal is a combination of the qualities that you admire most in other people. Since early childhood, you have been exposed through family, school, media, and life itself to qualities such as integrity, courage, wisdom, humility, compassion, love, and forgiveness. These qualities have been calibrated in your subconscious mind. Their importance in relation to each other creates an ideal of the best person you could be.

Where animals have a natural survival instinct, humans have a natural success instinct. Consciously or unconsciously, you continuously strive to live up to your ideal. The clearer you are about what that self-ideal is, the more likely you are to reach your goals in both your personal and work life. The test then centers on the degree to which your current behaviors and actions are congruent with your ideals.

Setting clear, written goals and acting on them is a big step towards attaining your self-ideal.

Closing the self-ideal gap starts with "imagineering." There are, of course, endless possibilities within your imagination. Who are your heroes? Your professional role models? Heroes can inspire you to become all that you aspire to be. Role models can show you what you need to do to achieve your goals. Let us look at both:

- Role models are people you can emulate. If you are in a position to work closely with them, so much the better. They do not have to be famous. The role models in your sector should have at least one talent that you have, be more proficient than you in one competency area, and be available on a regular basis so that you can watch them in action.
- Heroes or heroines differ from role models, but they can also help you clarify and work towards your self-ideal. Your heroes personify your values and ideals. They represent who you can become. A society writes its history by naming its heroes and glorifying their greatness.

Reading the autobiographies and biographies of great leaders and achievers—Gandhi, Mandela, Jesus, Napoleon, and Churchill—helps you compare their ideals and values with your own.

If you have no heroes or heroines, perhaps you have not identified your values or highest ideals. "Everyone is equal"—the common-man ethos—is a kind of antihero phase that societies go through periodically. It does not work. Your heroes or heroines take responsibility and accomplish things. They should inspire you. If you look up, you will be drawn up.

Having a magnificent obsession clarifies and brings focus to your self-ideal, which helps crystallize your self-image and raises your self-esteem. You can choose to make consulting a magnificent obsession.

Your Self-Image

Your self-image is your inner mirror. It is how you see and think about yourself, right now. You constantly "look" in this metaphorical mirror to check how you are doing physically, mentally, and emotionally. You use it to determine how you should respond to circumstances and people. It is your current reality checkpoint.

The key to self-image is "as within, so without." There is a perfect correspondence between your inner state of mind and your outer reactions and actions. You will always tend to live up to, or down to, your current assessment of yourself. Nowhere is this manifested more than in the level of fees you charge your clients. You can immediately see the connection with your self-ideal.

When you are clear, positive, and happy with your self-image, your performance goes up, your talents kick in, and your attitudes and interactions give you energy and creativity. When your self-image is poor, you experience stress, self-imposed inferiority, and envisage all the ways that things will fail to work out.

Your Self-Esteem

Your current reality, good or bad, is the sum of all the choices you have made. All choices have consequences, and these consequences go towards creating your self-image. Self-esteem is the barometer that shows how your self-image is moving towards or away from your self-ideal.

Self-esteem is your reputation with yourself. It is best measured by how much you accept, respect, and regard yourself as a valuable and worthwhile advisor. The higher your self-esteem, the happier, more enthusiastic, and productive you will be as a professional consultant.

Self-esteem is the foundation of personal growth, career development, and advisory achievement. It is also central in the development of peer-level respect with clients. Clients, consciously or subconsciously, often deal with advisors as a vendor or a mere supplier. Unfortunately, the majority of advisors allow this form of relationship to develop. They then suffer the consequences in ad hoc, low-impact assignments and of course, low fees, which in turn lower self-esteem. It can become a downward spiral. This is often the root cause for those who leave the profession.

Your positioning with the client as an advisor is as clear an indicator of your self-image as you can get. How you intend to reposition yourself is a factor of your self-ideal visualization. Your self-esteem is the key mechanism to trigger your mind-set and skill set changes to be the best consultant you can be and to fulfil your purpose.

Writing Your Personal Strategy

The primary objective of writing your personal strategy is to bring clarity and focus to who you are and what you do—in written format. There is a particular power in setting out your personal strategy in writing that you do not get if you merely imagine that strategy. For more guidance on this process, see our 2013 e-book, *Crossing the Rubicon: Seven Steps to Writing Your Own Personal Strategy*, which outlines the seven-step master formulation process in great detail.

When working with clients, the Odyssey consultant often recommends that each member of the client team work on their own personal strategic plan using the Rubicon process. The logic is that if you can think strategically for yourself, if you can understand who you are on the inside and what you want to do on the outside, you will be better positioned to create, understand, and implement the strategy for your organization.

A Word on Responsibility—A Consultant Obligation

Responsibility underpins your success as a consultant. Taking 100% responsibility and being accountable is absolutely critical to reaching your personal and professional potential and doing your very best work as an expert in your field.

The scope of responsibility begins with personal responsibility and broadens to client responsibility, corporate, community, and environmental responsibilities.

In his classic book, *The Seven Habits of Highly Effective People*, Stephen Covey states, "Proactive people recognize responsibility. They do not blame circumstances, conditions, or conditioning for their behavior. Their behavior is a product of their own conscious choice, based on values, rather than a product of their conditions, based upon feelings."

Responsibility is the willingness and the ability to respond and act positively to situations and human interactions. Personal responsibility is the ability to take charge of your own life.

The key to developing a great professional practice is to recognize your own responsibility mind-set. That is, your natural human tendency to justify, defend, and rationalize why you are not making the progress you know you could and should be making.

The first step towards taking full responsibility is to take the decision "to be" a successful professional advisor, "to have" the financial freedom that you deserve, and "to do" the kind of work that feeds your passion.

Professional responsibility means taking ownership, in a purposeful way, for the sequence of events in your professional life and career. Professional advisory responsibility means identifying your natural talents and mastering the competencies and consulting opportunities that flow from them. It is also about knowing your limitations.

Invest in Yourself

To reap the lucrative benefits of a high-fee practice, your first responsibility must be to invest in your self-development. This will require a paradigm shift for many advisors who think they are entitled to success based on their expertise, education, and experience. The people who can help you most in unblocking the professional dimension of your advisory career are the successful experts in your field. Connect with mastermind groups, find an accountability partner who will "tell it like it is," join the Odyssey MasterClass, or contract a coach.

One of our Odyssey graduates said recently, "Seeing the world from the desk as the contracted help is a giant leap from corporate responsibility to personal and professional responsibility. It requires a significant transition in thinking ... and acting."

Another graduate said, "Being an A1 consultant isn't easy. You have to be responsible for redesigning your career through a combination of new learning, new attitudes, new methods, new behaviors and feet on the street."

Two Reasons People Do Not Take Full Responsibility

Fear

Fear is a root cause of irresponsible behaviors. Fear prods at the very core of our own significance, vulnerabilities, helplessness, isolation, and fragility. The fact is that everyone is vulnerable. We are all conditioned from childhood with a variety of fears. It is the epicenter of much of our success deprivation. Fear cannot be denied. It is part of our humanness. We must acknowledge and recognize fear for what it is. We must manage it and consciously overcome it where possible.

- Ralph Waldo Emerson wrote, "Do the thing you fear and the death of fear is certain."
- Mark Twain wrote, "Courage is not lack of fear, absence of fear; it is control of fear, mastery of fear."

There is often a great irony present in consulting situations, particularly those on the human performance improvement side of the consulting equation. Helping clients overcome their limitations, challenges, and fears by advising and coaching does not necessarily mean you have met, overcome, or even addressed your own fear demons. Sometimes we teach what we most need to learn ourselves. Could it be fear around this process that is stopping you from charging higher fees?

Absence of Courage

Emotional courage is both the ability and the willingness to confront fear, uncertainty, and doubt. Moral courage is the ability to do the right thing in the face of popular opposition or opinion.

Lack of courage in your own life carries over to professional practice. As a consultant, you are called upon to have both emotional and moral courage, whether it be to buttress your point of view or recommend a particular solution, to say no to an assignment or person because that is the right thing to do or to end a consulting assignment at the right time. You are unlikely to challenge your client when you lack the courage of your own convictions.

Eight Courage-Creating Principles

1. Dream big dreams, assist clients to achieve their big dreams.
2. Face current realities, overcome self-limiting beliefs and fear.
3. Take 100% responsibility, be accountable, and stop managing blame.
4. Confront the challenges and circumstances, make decisions, and move on.
5. Invite and receive feedback, be vulnerable to constructive criticism.
6. Embrace learning, relearning, and unlearning.
7. Define and own your integrity, stand your moral ground.
8. *Carpe diem*—seize the day. Opportunities abound.

Consulting and Corporate Responsibility

When widespread wrongdoing is discovered in a corporate context, the questions always asked are as follows: How can a whole organization engage in fraud? Is there not one honest person in there? The answer is simple, but not obvious. When a culture of fear exists, the natural desire to "do the right thing" is neutralized. Personal responsibility gives way to fear and groupthink becomes the norm.

The goal of the advisor is to balance a drive for results while empowering people to do their best work. Only when a concern for people, values, and ethics is interwoven with the drive for productivity will a culture of corporate and social responsibility emerge.

Getting the responsibility formula right is often tightrope walk. Consultants can play a large role in helping leaders and organizations work towards this objective. The consultant must not be intimidated by the culture and should have little fear of asking the right questions or challenging inconsistencies in values within the scope of their consulting assignment.

A responsibility culture has a multitude of advantages when it comes to ensuring that consulting assignments are implemented. There is less stress so you can focus on creative problem solving, less staff turnover so you can allocate more time to key result areas, fewer problems because ownership is taken at source, less time lost doing the wrong things and more time to focus on performance improvement differentiators, strategy, and execution.

The field of corporate responsibility has grown exponentially in the last decade, primarily because there is a growing body of data—quantitative and qualitative—that demonstrates the bottom-line benefits of socially responsible, people-first corporate performance. Similarly, conscious capitalism is an emerging business movement that is attracting attention and gathering momentum in the corporate context. It behoves the consultant to become well versed in values and corporate responsibility models.

Timeless Life and Consulting Principles

A principle is a fundamental truth that forms the basis for solid reasoning and making sound judgment calls. Consultants and individuals alike have discovered that health, wealth, and happiness come from living in harmony with four timeless principles. They are as relevant today as they were thousands of years ago. They are neutral, unemotional, and operate universally. While the world changes, they remain unchanged.

Consistently ignoring these principles in your personal and professional life will hinder your progress and success. However, if you work with them, they help facilitate the achievement of your ultimate objectives in life; they will help you reach your full potential in your consulting business. Living in congruence with these principles gives you control of the direction of your life and business.

Here are the "Big 4" timeless principles for you to consider:

1. The timeless principle of cause and effect
2. The timeless principle of belief
3. The timeless principle of expectation
4. The timeless principle of attraction

The Timeless Principle of Cause and Effect

There is a cause for every effect in the universe, a reason for every consequence in your life. Earlier choices (or nonchoices) predict present outcomes. There are no accidents. Nothing happens on its own.

Aristotle (384–322 BC), a Greek philosopher, educator, and scientist, was one of the greatest and most influential thinkers in Western culture and is regarded as one of the first to write about the timeless principle of cause and effect. In the bible, the principle is referenced as follows: "Whatsoever a man soweth, that also shall he reap." In scientific terms, Sir Isaac Newton called it the third principle of motion: "For every action, there is an equal and opposite reaction." In modern terms, we define your attitude or mind-set as "the cause" and your reality or outcome as "the effect." To put it simply, if you keep doing what you are doing, you will only get more of what you already have.

This principle is psychological in nature, in that a thought triggers every action, positive or negative. You make it work in your consulting life by developing a higher sense of awareness and understanding of how your mind processes things. In so doing, you begin to take control of the causes (inputs) and therefore the effects (outputs) in terms of your achievements, success, happiness, and prosperity. When you are absolutely clear about what outcomes and goals you want, you can work on the reasons (causes) for ensuring that a successful outcome (effect) takes place. You work on invoking best practice in whatever area of endeavor you desire a positive effect.

What does that mean in terms of your consulting business? It means that success and failure are predictable. If you can cause enough positive effects to happen, you will be successful.

Learning to understand the conditioning process that determines your attitude and how your mind works is critical to tapping into the timeless principle of cause and effect. Your mind-set and thoughts (causes) trigger your emotions and words that, in turn, lead to your actions and consequent outcomes (effects). You change your current realities by tracing back the original reasons or causes that led you towards the right or wrong choices. You begin to change your future by triggering positive forms of cause.

Cause and effect may not always be close together in space and time. Today's problems frequently arise as a result of yesterday's choices, which means that the rot in thinking is usually well advanced before the condition manifests itself. If you want something to happen, you have to cause it to happen. You have a choice. The effects are the consequences. This is the power of the principle.

All of those who attend Odyssey programs do so with good intentions. They are motivated and have signaled they want either to become consultants or to be more effective as consultants. Next comes the work required to inventory their talent and change their mind-set. Through the process, they leave the old behind and begin internalizing the new. The MasterClass is the transformational stage where the new consultant identity emerges. They are now ready to apply this newfound identity in the real world.

Personal mastery and creating business advantage must be activity oriented. Neither setting objectives nor making commitments actually make anything happen. Only activities or specific next moves improve the odds of achieving those results, allowing those activities to be designated as causes and the results as effects.

As one graduate said, "I got Odyssey conceptually-process and methodology, it took longer than expected to make it work in practice … but I persevered and it worked and is working. Without the experience I would still be trying to do what I have always done"—cause and effect in action.

A Practical Example

Here is a practical, seven-step, systematic problem-solving sequence, which many consultants apply, with particular emphasis on cause and effect. Its purpose is to produce creative solutions within your own consulting practice and while working with clients.

Step 1: Clarify the effects of the problem
   Always start by defining the effect. Ask, "Is there a problem?" "What is the problem?" "What are its effects?" Be specific. Quantify it. Gather the facts. Resist the temptation to go for an early solution. Using your personal competencies, experiences, expertise, and training, ask, "What are the present effects?" "What are the long-term effects?" "How does the problem affect the big picture?" "How much does it cost?"

Step 2: Identify the root causes of the problem
   For a consultant to understand and solve a client's business problems, it is critical that you understand the causes. Root cause analysis using Fishbone diagrams is one technique

   – To discover the root cause of a problem,
   – To uncover bottlenecks in processes,
   – To identify where and why a process is not working.

Step 3: Generate possible solutions
   There are several creative-thinking techniques to generate ideas and solutions to solve the clearly defined problem. Remember that creativity is the thinking process that helps generate ideas, and innovation is the application of these ideas with the aim of doing things better, faster, cheaper, and more easily. Creative-thinking techniques include brainstorming, mind mapping, lateral thinking, brain writing, problem gallery, story boarding, and the twenty-idea method.

Step 4: Select the best solution

It is important to identify the one best solution that inevitably emerges. This is not to say that all other ideas are cast aside. They can be organized on an ideas board under different themes and retained for future reference.

Step 5: Implement decisions

The key question is, What action is to be taken? This allows the leader to set SMART (specific, measurable, achievable, realistic, and time-bounded) goals. Remember that while creativity is the start, real innovation lies in implementation, which is the effective result.

Step 6: Assign responsibility for the outcome

When working with a client, you must ensure that someone takes overall responsibility for the implementation of the action steps/plans. Do not assume or expect that everyone will just execute the actions outlined. No matter how enthusiastic they are or how much they promise, unless you get actual commitment, nothing will happen. This is why the name or names of individuals should always be written into the plan. One person who commits their name to the outcome is better than twenty enthusiastic group members. As a consultant, keeping clients committed to their "promises to themselves" can be one of your most valuable contributions.

Step 7: Agree reporting and feedback procedure

"What gets measured, gets done" is a solid management principle. Agreement on a reporting and feedback procedure is a critical factor in locking in the individuals responsible for taking action. It is also vital for the upkeep of motivation among group members who contributed to the earlier part of the process. Clarify how outcomes will be communicated back to the main group and set out a schedule showing when this will take place. Without this step in the process, cynicism will infect all future creative thinking initiatives.

The Timeless Principle of Belief

The timeless principle of belief simply states that your beliefs determine your actions and therefore your life outcomes.

Beliefs are like filters that screen out information that is inconsistent with them. You tend to reject information that contradicts what you have already decided to believe, whether that information is true or false.

During your early years, you were exposed to a multitude of influences that lead you to accept, as true, certain things that you classify as beliefs. These belief systems determine your perceptions of both your internal life and your world view. Some beliefs may have served you well; others may hinder your future progress.

Because beliefs cause you to think in a particular way, you will sometimes ignore or filter out valuable information. You literally develop a "blind spot," or a psychological scotoma to certain realities, opportunities, and possibilities. For a consultant, it is important to carefully guard against these blind spots, which may prompt you to jump to the wrong conclusions about yourself and your clients.

A negative belief system is like a self-imposed brake on your natural talents and core competencies. Of these negative beliefs, self-limiting beliefs are among the most damaging. They prevent you from tapping into your inherent power and from using your inborn talents, values, and attributes. Self-limiting beliefs stop your behaviors, talents, emotional intelligence, and attitudes from combining to become strengths and superior competencies. Here are some examples:

- I realize I did fairly well, but I absolutely should have done perfectly on a task like this, and therefore I really am incompetent.
- I know what will happen because of what has happened before.
- I do not deserve to be wealthy.

Stereotyping is another example of how the negative side of the belief principle is manifested. Stereotyping has many names: labelling, classifying, typecasting, pigeonholing, and prejudging. It stems from deeply held preconvictions and in essence, it is about a failure to see individuals and situations for who and what they are. Do not allow yourself to be stereotyped as "just a consultant." Be careful that you do not unwittingly take on the "sins of the father," or the impressions left by novice consultants or clients who set the bar low.

You tend to act in a manner consistent with your beliefs, and that is especially true of beliefs that relate to you. The primary reason a client does not "go with you" on an assignment—all else being equal—is that they do not believe you. If you do not believe in yourself, your client will intuit this and fail to believe you.

Mankind has been testing the principle of belief for more than 2,000 years.

- In the Old Testament, it says, "As a man thinketh in his heart, so is he."
- The New Testament says, "According to your faith, be it done unto you."
- Nietzsche wrote, "He who has a why to live can bear almost any how."
- Allen James wrote, "Men do not attract that which they *want,* but that which they *are.*"
- Shakespeare wrote, "Nothing is but thinking makes it so."

Dr. Viktor Frankl spent three years in Auschwitz prison. He sums up the principle of belief in his book *Man's Search for Meaning* as follows: "In the concentration camp, what remains with you is the last of the human freedoms—the ability to choose your attitude in a given set of circumstances."

The Performance Improvement Loop

The performance improvement loop shows how your beliefs trigger your attitudes and behaviors, which in turn lead to the results you get (Figure 6.7). These results, good or bad, reinforce what you believe, and so the loop—either positive or negative—continues.

Your "reality" is filtered through your five senses and your belief system to deliver your perception. The five senses are also the window to your sixth sense, your intuition, your inner voice. Your senses interpret, collate, and act as gatekeeper to your beliefs, while perception is the process of creating your picture of the world around you, one which is filtered through your beliefs.

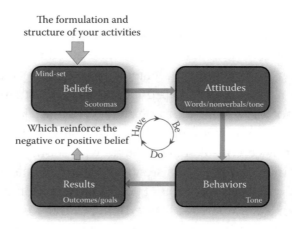

Figure 6.7   The performance improvement loop.

Three Considerations for Assimilating Experiences

People tend to become prisoners of their experiences. You organize and interpret information according to what has happened to you in the past. There are three considerations here:

1. Everything is relative

    Your perceptions as a consultant are relative to the situations in which they occur. When you find yourself in unfamiliar surroundings, you no longer have the references on which to base your perception. For example, how expensive is an expensive assignment? To an economic buyer with a discretionary budget of $1,000,000 or a manager with a budget of $20,000? How fast is fast to a CEO with a five-year growth strategy or an HR manager with a training need next month? The consultant may project a previous fee setting experience on the next assignment, making untested assumptions about the client's needs, budget, or willingness to engage. Check your perceptions and assumptions and treat each case as unique.

2. The tendency to generalize

    You have a natural inclination to generalize based on your previous experiences. You may tend to pinpoint certain features of an upcoming assignment and then go on to make sweeping generalizations about the boundaries and limitations of the assignment. Remember, all assignments are different. Do not allow yourself to become complacent and a victim of generalization.

3. Your personality influences

    Your temperament, personal interests, attitudes, and values "flavor" your perception. So does your lifetime journey, education, and learning. Your beliefs determine how you interpret or explain things to yourself. Consider the following example.

    A consultant is overheard talking with another consultant. Consultant one says, "I don't consult to manufacturing enterprises. They are dirty, unsafe and the people there leave a lot to be desired." The second consultant responds, "Manufacturing consulting makes up 47% of my revenue. I would rethink your thoughtware on this one."

    Remember that learned frames of mind can be changed and unlearned. You are free to choose. As a professional consultant, consider these two questions:

a. What are your core beliefs that have served you well to this point in your consulting career?
b. What are the self-limiting beliefs that may not be helping you achieve your full potential?

In answering these questions, it is important to have good quality feedback from a professional mentor/coach or someone who knows you well.

The Timeless Principle of Expectation

The timeless principle of expectation says that your major assumptions, hopes, desires, and predominant thoughts tend to become self-fulfilling prophecies. Your relative levels of optimism and pessimism have a powerful effect on what you achieve. Setting clear, positive expectations for yourself and others acts as an organizing principle in how worthwhile things get done. Having unclear, low, or no expectations inevitably leads to low performance and an unsuccessful outcome. If you do not know where you are going, any road will lead you there.

As a professional advisor, expectations management is vital to reaching the top echelons of the consulting business, and all expectations start with the expectations you have of yourself. In turn, the environment you create for your clients sets their expectations of the work you will do together.

Sport often provides good metaphors. One team expects to win their championship as if it were their moral right ... another team believes its destiny is simply to compete and play well. In the majority of cases like this, both expectations are met.

Your ability to learn how to set and achieve goals is the single most important means of capitalizing on your expectations. Disciplining your clients to stick to their commitments through explicit expectations can be the most valuable gift you can give them.

The two fundamental preconditions to anchor any work on expectation management are as follows:

1. Trust

Trust is your willingness to be vulnerable to someone else's actions, based on your understanding that their actions are important to you. Do not confuse trust with risk and cooperation. We all know in our hearts what it means to trust someone, and almost everyone knows how it feels to have that trust betrayed. Why do you trust one person, but not another? And how do you behave differently towards someone you trust versus someone you do not? Without an element of trust, how could you take on an assignment, make a contract for services, or make appointments? With trust, you enter into friendships, marriage, partnerships, and consulting agreements. Clearly, trust and its cousin trustworthiness are the essential ingredients in setting and meeting expectations.

2. Effective communication

Effective communication is all about listening, observing, questioning, verifying, and explaining (all learnable skills) to bring clarity to the various roles and goals within a client organization. Errant assumptions are the root cause of most misunderstandings, communication breakdowns, stress, and frustration within any group of people. Unfortunately, many consultants do not formally clarify or discuss expectations around an engagement, which often results in grey areas emerging during the project. This oversight can then go on to sabotage the overall outcome. It is important that the consultant sets up a forum to discuss unmet expectations and any "undiscussables."

Conflicting Expectations

The exceptional consultant understands that conflicting expectations manifest themselves at all levels of society, business, and life.

As high as 70% of all mergers and acquisitions fail over time because the key participants engage in hard financial numbers negotiation on a win–lose or lose–win basis. The legal and financial merger becomes an end game in itself, and minimal consideration is given to the human and cultural merger that must also take place. When two cultures come together, new understandings and expectations must be clarified, or a clash of wills is inevitable. Expectations management is what makes the merger work after the merger sign off. This is bread and butter territory for a consultant.

Expectations in relationships and personal partnerships have changed dramatically over the years. At the same time, implicit expectations around the roles of partners vary significantly depending on the context. A multitude of expectations are evident in a personal relationship and family situation.

Parents' expectations—perceived or actual—make one of the most powerful psychological impressions on life choices and career path development. To what degree are your parents' expectations of you—perhaps set decades ago—determining your ceiling as a consultant? One Odyssey candidate told us, "My mom and dad programmed me for hard work, not smart work. I find myself measuring success from the hours I put in, whether they generate value or not."

Expectations about yourself represent one of the most powerful manifestations of this principle. Certain fundamental expectations are essential to successful consulting competency. These essentials include high levels of self-confidence, self-responsibility, self-respect, and self-actualization.

Key influencers, such as teachers and supervisors, can have a lifelong, profound effect on the scope of your self-fulfilling prophesies as a consultant—if you let them. We tend to build expectations around what the boss expects us to do. If we are not careful, we let the client become our new boss, and this limits the relationship to this mode of interaction. For mutual benefit, the client–consultant relationship needs to be a peer-level relationship based on mutual respect and trust.

An organization's expectations may center on productivity, a psychological or cultural buy-in, and a sense of loyalty to the objectives of the organization. However, the expectations between client and consultant are not always clear. When implicit or explicit expectations are broken, there is inevitably a ripple effect of adverse consequences. Whenever different departments, teams, or people from different disciplines interface, you can expect conflicting expectations.

Meeting and exceeding expectations has been the customer service mantra for more than a decade. Delivering outstanding customer care can only happen if deep-seated cultural principles are present in the organization. Loudly proclaiming, in promotional or marketing campaigns, that "we are the best" and "the customer is king" can have a boomerang effect if the expectations of customer and company are mismatched. This is fallow ground for the consultant, who can assist in the embedding of values and customer service delivery practices.

"Under promise and overdeliver" is a powerful way of managing client expectations. For example, if you promise to deliver a proposal by Friday and do so on Monday, your client will be disappointed. If you deliver it on Thursday, you have risen in their estimation.

Consultants often feel the pressure to promise and get caught up in urgency mode, although, in fact, rapid delivery may not be necessary. Consulting propositions are rarely life-or-death scenarios and, in fact, often benefit from gestation time.

Broken promises shatter trust, and trust is an essential ingredient of expectations management. Conflicting expectations around goals and roles is a major cause of ineffective or poor performance consulting.

Four Possible Causes of and Solutions to Unclear Expectations

There are four possible causes of unclear expectations that lead to under-performance in any consulting situation. Each expectation shortfall can be solved by a different competency solution or practice, as follows:

1. The consultant is unclear about what is expected of them in a client-facing role.

   They have not considered the boundaries of the consulting profession for themselves, or how to contract properly with their client. Always determine the scope of the project with absolute clarity.

2. The consultant is unaware that they are not meeting expectations.

   They are blissfully soldiering on, and neither client nor consultant raises the issue. Learning to ask for and receive feedback is the solution to this expectation gap. To restate, feedback is the breakfast of champions.

3. The consultant is unable to meet expectations.

   The complexity of the problem, as it unfolds, may be different than diagnosed, or perhaps external factors have arisen, which materially change the issue. The solution here lies in acceptance of that fact and then disclosing it fully to the client. New consultants frequently try to be all things to all people, and overstretch or misdiagnose.

4. The consultant and the client may lock horns because of lack of clarity around approach or best outcomes.

   The courage to engage in a conflict with your client is the measure of how far you have come as a consultant. Some consultants underperform for the client and themselves simply because they like harmony and are afraid of tackling relationship issues. Weak relationships always live ten-tatively, and mediocrity is the inevitable result. The advice is to be brave; name the true issues and invite the client to engage in a workable solution.

Implicit and Explicit Expectations

Expectations can be broken into two distinct areas. Implicit expectations relate to psychological issues, and explicit expectations relate more to performance and career factors.

Implicit expectations are your unspoken hopes of, or desired outcomes from, a client assignment. Often, an implicit expectation is an imaginary map or a projection of how things should be.

Explicit expectations are usually defined in written form, such as legal contracts, key performance indicators, or some form of feedback loop. Like all contractual obligations, they are negotiable and are generally entered into freely by both parties.

Your primary task as a consultant is to meet and then exceed clients' expectations. When you manage expectations successfully, you influence how your client collaborates with you.

The Timeless Principle of Attraction

The principle suggests that your predominant attitudes attract into your life a sequence of events, circumstances, and people that reflect those attitudes. In other words, birds of a feather flock together. Everything seems to start with your thoughts, which trigger your feelings, which, in turn, lead to your words and actions. This inevitably leads to recurring patterns of behavior and outcomes.

How does it work? Your thoughts have a mental energy that you transmit in the form of body language, tone, words, and movement. However, on a psychological level, this transmission is even more powerful in that it seems to connect with others who are like you. This principle links perfectly with the principles of expectation and belief.

Here are two key factors related to attraction:

1. The halo effect

    Coined by psychologist Edward Thorndike in the 1920s, the halo effect is a positive judgment based on a single, dominant aspect of your personality, such as your speech, dress, posture, or behavior.

2. Stereotyping

    The second factor is stereotyping, a term first used by Walter Lippman, also in the 1920s. It captures the tendency for your client to group you with all other consultants who seem to have similar characteristics as you. The mental construct or picture in their head gets triggered when they meet a consultant. This overgeneralization is bound to be wrong at times and tends to be more negative than positive. Your challenge is to be different enough to be distinctive and "attractive."

Great Consulting Mind-Sets

- "Being" a great consultant is your own personal mind-set challenge.
- "Doing" what is necessary to be a great consultant is a learned competency.
- "Having" personal consulting revenues in the top 5% plus category is the result of the "being" and "doing" steps.

Is this the classic chicken and the egg dilemma? Which comes first, "being" the great consultant, "doing" the activities necessary, or "having" the million dollar personal revenues?

First, make a decision "to be" a great consultant. Learning how "to be" is a fundamental commitment to being the best in your field. You deserve to be everything you can possibly be. Decide.

Second, dedicate yourself to learn how "to do" the practices necessary to achieve consulting excellence. Learn the consulting models and how to acquire the portfolio of solutions that allow you to leverage yourself into the high-income consulting bracket. Learn.

Third, "having" an independent consulting practice that generates excellent personal revenues on a consistent basis is the result of being that great consultant in your field and doing the appropriate activities.

Top performing consultants think differently. This allows them to charge higher fees because they appreciate the real worth of their own contribution and bask in the glow that benefits from their advice and expertise.

Odyssey in Action I

Kathleen Caldwell, Caldwell Consulting Group, Woodstock, Illinois

Making Change Stick

When I go into a client workplace, the first thing I do is analyze the current situation with the team. What are they experiencing in their daily work? Almost always, there is inconsistency with results, skepticism about change, and more work with less satisfaction.

It's all about understanding their current reality. I do individual, anonymous surveys and then instigate a group session to begin the process of telling the truth about their experiences in the organization.

By saying "Look, what we're trying to do is make the workplace great," you're giving people a common goal.

In these sessions, the first thing you'll discover is a sense of commonality between the team members: "Wow, I didn't know that is how you feel!" It's vital of course that the ground rules are set. There's no defensiveness, no accusations flying. They're just bringing concepts up, getting it all out there. Our intention is to find ways to work better together.

At that session, I gather a long list of what's working, what's not working, and what could work better, and write it up on whiteboards. Typically, you'll find plenty of things that are working: There are good people with good intentions, there are good products, and there are good clients and customers. And, on the other side, you'll hear things like "There's too much gossip … not enough communication … the rules keep changing …"

With one recent client, there had been a lot of internal communication and morale issues. In particular, intense animosity had sprung up between two departments. Deadlines were being missed, and instead of taking responsibility, the staff were blaming the other side. These issues had reached a point where they were stressing the entire organization. People were getting caught in the crossfire and were being forced to take sides. Ultimately, it began to impact the company's ability to produce new products and meet revenue targets.

My intervention began by helping people to understand their role in creating and solving the situation. I worked with both teams to try to create more compassion and forgiveness for those on the other side, using an exercise that I call "Just Like Me." It's a way to break down the barriers and bring people to an understanding of those they're in conflict with. They're human beings too. They're doing the best they can.

This assignment was a real challenge. It took about two months before there was any significant change at all on either side.

Every organization is different, and the rate at which change happens depends so much on willingness. This gets back to the Odyssey concept, the necessity of there being a willingness and an openness to change. Making change stick and having a really high-performing organization took a full year, all four seasons.

How do we know it's working? We survey throughout the process. It's about people evaluating themselves and the team: On a scale of 0 to 10, how would you rate our ability to communicate effectively? How would you rate our ability to deal with difficult issues?

We're also tracking their new behaviors and their outcomes. What real results are happening within the organization? What's happening to them personally? What are they able to do that they couldn't do before? What are the new actions they're taking and what are the new results that they're getting?

And although the transformation process takes a year, it doesn't stop there. I'll continue to go back to that workplace on a semimonthly or quarterly basis, and I'll continue coaching and making sure that the initiatives that we introduced are effective and making a positive difference.

Much of my work is about helping people to set and maintain higher standards. For so many people, they've just lost their vision for themselves and for their work. Part of what I do is reinspiring and helping reignite their personal and professional vision. I show them how to get back to work and enjoy it.

Odyssey in Action II

John Oakes, CEO, SBL Consulting Group, Redding, California

Every Client Experience Is a Growth Opportunity

I was engaged by this client to develop a program to improve the performance of their store managers, and to create bench strength; turnover was a significant problem.

They asked me to come up with a plan to try to deepen the bench and develop quality people that were a good fit, thereby reducing costly turnover while at the same time enhancing leadership performance.

After several meetings spent gathering critical intel, it soon became evident that this was not the only issue. I conducted several Business Management Reviews (BMRs) with the CEO and his senior leadership team, after which I made a recommendation that the first step should be a three-day strategic planning retreat at an offsite location. The CEO admitted that they hadn't done any strategic planning in the company in some years, but he was open to the idea.

The BMRs exposed some serious culture issues and deficiencies at the leadership level. These would have to be dealt with before we could address his primary concern, which, as I say, was store manager quality and turnover. At that strategic retreat, I was able to uncover several organizational gaps and some legacy issues that were negatively impacting the overall performance of the company.

The CEO began to see that he was carrying out responsibilities that should have been delegated to others, and that one of his senior staff was not performing in his key role. This exec was also undermining the culture of the organization due to his negativism.

Another finding was that a number of executives couldn't define their own jobs. The CEO was a very bright and competent person, but the truth was that he didn't hold his leadership team to high levels of standards and accountability.

The biggest issue, however, is related to the CEO's number two. As we began to develop strategic initiatives, one of which addressed the store manager turnover problem, this executive simply didn't want to get involved. He had been in the company for thirty years. He was conservative, comfortable, and utterly unwilling to engage the obvious issues, preferring instead to simply maintain status quo.

As part of this strategic process, I began asking critical role-defining questions. The CEO began to see the critical issues more clearly, and he began to see that the number-two guy didn't have the capacity and vision to execute these issues effectively.

The week following, I was back in the CEO's office, having a discussion about my findings. Once we had gone through all of the issues, I asked him a question: "Knowing what you know now, would you hire your number two person for that role today?"

He looked at me intently. "No," he said, "not at all."

"Well," I said, "then you know what to do."

Sixty days later, the individual was out of the company.

The emotional culture of the organization began to change almost immediately. It's astonishing the negative impact a single individual can have on a leadership team.

So much of the process of making change lies in establishing responsibility and accountable commitments.

The CEO has achieved huge personal growth over the last two and a half years. Why? Because he's taking responsibility for things that he should have taken responsibility for before. The company has changed in a number of areas. "Succession by design" and consistent strategic processing have been implemented at every level in the organization.

I've been working with the CEO now for over two years. We meet once a month for two hours and we look at strategies to move the company forward, and it has moved forward phenomenally. I also meet with the senior leadership team monthly to stay in touch with the key initiatives.

The culture has been transformed. When I started there, sales were $145 million and value per share was $30. Today, its sales are approaching nearly $200 million and value per share is at $55. This is an ESOP company, an employee-owned company, so those numbers are a huge motivator. The people working there see that growth in share value and they will say, "I'll do anything it takes to make this company successful!"

In order to deal with the turnover problem, the company created a series of "On Deck" programs to source and retain managerial talent in each of the units. The two division managers have taken ownership of "On Deck," which is now in its third iteration. The quality of the people who are coming into and working their way through the program is outstanding. We have millennials, along with more experienced people, but those who come through it are really excited about the opportunity; people want to be in the program because they really feel they can make a contribution to the company. This provides them with a career path that did not exist previously.

Working with the company has really allowed me to grow personally as well. Every client experience is a growth opportunity. It is a reminder to listen well, to ask the key questions, to interpret the real issues, and to guide the client down a path of self-discovery. I don't try to teach them as much as to encourage them to start to teach themselves. If you have the right people in the right place, doing the right things, you'll get the right results, and you will facilitate one of the most meaningful processes of discovery and change that can happen.

Chapter Summary

The chapter begins by examining the nature of success before going on to discuss the six dimensions of total success. In understanding the consultant's mind-set, the triple mind looks at the classic division of mind function into conscious, subconscious, and superconscious and demonstrates how present moment awareness is a key learnable skill for personal mastery in the profession of consulting.

Next, we looked at recent developments in positive psychology and explored the key topics of self-ideal, self-image, and self-esteem. Understanding the responsibility issue is fundamental to all consulting mind-sets. The related discipline of business consulting responsibility has broadened considerably in recent years and is an area of particular interest for consultants. Finally, we explore four timeless life and consulting principles.

Calls to Action

1. What steps can you take to further integrate the talent management model into your life and consulting business?

   _____
   _____
   _____
   _____
   _____
   _____
   _____
   _____

2. How are you currently rating yourself on the six dimensions of success? What steps are you planning to develop your success map?

   _____
   _____
   _____
   _____
   _____
   _____
   _____
   _____

3. How is your triple mind serving you (i.e., your conscious mind, your subconscious mind, and your superconscious mind)? What steps are you planning to develop them?

   _____
   _____
   _____
   _____
   _____
   _____
   _____
   _____

4. Your self-concept: How positive is your self-ideal, your self-image, and your self-esteem? Set out your positive action steps to make improvements in your business and personal life. Be precise.

_____

_____

_____

_____

_____

_____

_____

_____

5. Which of the four timeless life and consulting principles is your strong point? Which is your identified area for development? Name planned actions.

_____

_____

_____

_____

_____

_____

_____

_____

_____

Bibliography

Allen, J. (2007). *As a Man Thinketh*. New York: Dover Publications.

Barrett, R. (2014). *The Values-Driven Organization: Unleashing Human Potential for Performance and Profit*. New York: Routledge.

Buckingham, M., & Coffman, C. (1999). *First, Break All the Rules: What the World's Greatest Managers Do Differently*. New York: Simon & Schuster.

Butler, I. (2013). *Crossing the Rubicon: Seven Steps to Writing Your Own Personal Strategy*. Dublin: Century Management.

Butler-Bowden, T. (2007). *50 Psychology Classics*. London: Nicholas Brealey Publishing.

Ciarrochi, J. (2013). *Mindfulness, Acceptance, and Positive Psychology: The Seven Foundations of Well-Being*. Oakland, CA: Context Press.

Compton, W. C., & Hoffman, E. (2012). *Positive Psychology: The Science of Happiness and Flourishing* (2nd ed.). Belmont, CA: Wadsworth Publishing.

Covey, S. R. (2004). *The 7 Habits of Highly Effective People: Powerful Lessons in Personal Change*. New York: Simon & Schuster.

Covey, S. M. R. (2008). *The SPEED of Trust: The One Thing That Changes Everything*. New York: Simon & Schuster.

Dalai Lama, & Van den Muyzenberg, L. (2008). *The Leader's Way*. London: Nicholas Brealey Publishing.

Fischer, J. (2006). *Navigating the Growth Curve*. Boulder, CO: Growth Curve Press.

Frankl, V. E. (2006). *Man's Search for Meaning*. Boston, MA: Beacon Press.

Hartman, L., DesJardins, J., & MacDonald, C. (2013). *Business Ethics: Decision Making for Personal Integrity & Social Responsibility*. New York: McGraw-Hill.

Kennedy, S. S. (2014). *Seasons of Hope*. London: The Random House Group Limited.

Lencioni, P. (2001). *Getting Naked*. San Francisco: Jossey Bass.

Mackey, J., & Sisodia, R. (2014). *Conscious Capitalism: Liberating the Heroic Spirit of Business*. Boston, MA: Harvard Business School Publishing Corporation.

McGraw, P. (2001). *Self Matters: Creating Your Life from the Inside Out*. New York: Simon & Schuster.

Peters, S. (2012). *The Chimp Paradox: The Mind Management Programme*. London, England: Penguin Publishing.

Sandberg, S., & Scovell, N. (2013). *Lean in*. New York: Knopf.

Schwartz, J. M., & Begley, S. (2003). *The Mind and the Brain: Neuroplasticity and the Power of Mental Force*. New York: HarperCollins.

Sharma, R. S. (1997). *The Monk Who Sold His Ferrari*. New York: HarperCollins.

Staub, R. (1999). *7 Acts of Courage: Living Your Life Wholeheartedly*. Provo, UT: Executive Excellence Publishing.

Tolle, E. (1999). *The Power of Now*. Vancouver: Namaste Publishing.

Tolle, E. (2006). *A New Earth: Awakening to Your Life's Purpose*. New York: Penguin Publishing.

Walsch, N. D. (2009). *When Everything Changes, Change Everything: In a Time of Turmoil, a Pathway to Peace*. Charlottesville, VA: Hampton Roads Publishing Company, Inc.

Chapter 7

Odyssey Reflections

Odyssey graduates talk about their experience in the Odyssey program and the impact it has had on their lives, both business and personal.

John Butler and Getting Out of Your Own Way

Dr. Shayne Tracy, CEO, Executive Strong, Ontario, Canada

The genesis of Odyssey occurred for me in 2005 at the annual TTI Conference in Phoenix, Arizona. I attended the plenary session to hear the late John Butler speak on the topic of "Odyssey: The Business of Consulting."

John Butler was a visionary, a Level 4 Master Practitioner and a "consultant's consultant." He saw the need for individual consultants to develop what he called "the business of consulting."

He said, "It's difficult to consult to a business owner if you are not a business yourself. If you are not investing in yourself and your business, how can you expect a business to invest in you and your business?"

I had been consulting since 1990, but on reflection, I realized that I had not been in *the business* of consulting. I told myself that I was running a business, but in reality Dr. Shayne Tracy was practicing what he knew best from his experience, which was performance management, strategic planning, assessment, coaching, and leadership development.

Sitting in that session that day, I become increasingly uneasy, not least because self-doubt and persistent uneasiness had been there in the background for some time. This self-doubt was a symptom of the "impostor syndrome." Those afflicted remain convinced that they are frauds and do not deserve the success that they have achieved.

As I listened to John that day, much of what he said challenged my personal status quo. I had been associated with the TTI organization for a decade or more and was using their well-researched assessment tools for leadership training, coaching, teambuilding, and hiring in a variety of organizational development applications. I was making a good living but the gnawing reality of the moment whispered to me that it was not a great living.

I would come to know what a great living meant through the Odyssey process.

John Butler's presentation was a resounding wake-up call. I was doing Level 1 and some Level 2 work, but not Level 3 or 4 consulting. John was a forthright presenter and a forthright person; what you saw and heard is what you got. He did not mince his words and implored all of us in the room to rethink our purpose, our so-called consulting business, and what stage we were at in that business.

I left the session with mixed emotions. I knew that I had to change something, but I was not quite sure what that was. I knew that I was doing good work, for the most part, and that I was having an impact on my clients. I knew that I delivered results and that I had creative solutions. However, the key thing I took away from John's presentation was this: I realized that I didn't feel that my clients really *appreciated* what I had to offer. In fact, the underlying emotion, to be completely honest, was one of rejection. I felt my self-worth was constantly being challenged, and that was reflected in my fees and billings.

I thought about why I had chosen consulting as a career. I had many of the perks that most people would give anything to enjoy. I had freedom of time, opportunities to work on my own without a boss, and good open-ended income opportunities. I had been given the opportunity to learn new practices and techniques, I'd met a wide variety of interesting people, and I got time off to enjoy treasured vacations and travel, time to manage family, and personal affairs. Last but not least, it gave me the passion and purpose to make a difference in the world.

Not long after John's presentation, I bumped up against him in the conference hall. I said politely, "I enjoyed your presentation; it gave much to think about."

He immediately said, in his assertive Irish brogue, "So what are you going to do about it? You need to get with the program!" I mumbled a couple of words without a committed answer. He said, as only John could say it, "Talk is cheap. Actions make things happen … Get on with it!"

This was more powerful input for me to think about and, more particularly, to feel about. My head said, "Let me take a rational approach to this." My heart said, after I had overcome the inner critic who rears its ugly head when one is most vulnerable, "Stop thinking you know it all. It's time to seriously examine what you are doing. It's time to stop feeling less than who you are, and above all, it is time to ensure your clients pay for the value you provide."

I debated with myself about the cost-benefit of signing up to Odyssey, and in the end said—somewhat arrogantly—"I am doing it! I must invest in myself to be the best I can be!" I hadn't known that there was a way to develop, build, or grow my consulting business. I was loaded up with academic credentials but not a speck of consulting education or training. I asked myself the question John had posited during his talk, "If I don't do this, how can I ask others to invest or pay me for what I do?"

So, I signed up for the Odyssey program.

A client was referred to me when I was working on the second module. The company was a small biotech. Among other things, they wanted me to conduct an organizational review and deliver findings on position descriptions, performance appraisal, organizational charts, staff engagement, and leadership development. I conducted my first M1 and M1r and had an abbreviated BMR with the CEO and board chairman.

When I reached the REC stage, I wrote up my proposal and began setting out the fee structure. As I did, the old emotional reminders resurfaced: "You need the money, don't lose this opportunity … you will feel really bad if you lose this contract … other consultants out there will charge less … you might need to lowball this fee to get the work … they don't really need *you* to do this … do you think the CEO and board chair really like you or know what you can do … or really care?"

With the strength of what I knew and had experienced from my short time with the Odyssey process, I gritted my teeth and doubled my fee. As I wrote the numbers into the proposal, as tough as it was, I said, "I am worth every dollar because I know I will deliver ten times the value to the organization!"

And that's exactly what happened. What a rewarding affirmation that was! I was now in a different place, with an entirely different mind-set.

As I reflect today on my Odyssey experience, it has changed both my life and my work. As a consultant, there must be a conscious integration of who you are and what you do. To be successful requires a full appreciation, understanding, and, above all, an opportunity to combine and integrate being with doing. Odyssey is my true opportunity for life–work integration.

Harking back to that day in Phoenix, let me share the eight lessons from John Butler that continue to resonate with me to this day:

1. Get yourself out of the way. You must be courageous and a risk taker to have life–work integration. Your talent and solutions are worth more than most consultants believe they can charge for them. Most have feelings of low self-worth and tend to leave money on the table.
2. You are a business and a profession that makes a difference. Your business must show profit, and your profession must deliver results for you and the client.
3. Give up the "commodities" mind-set in providing services; the client can't buy it from anyone else if you have developed a value-based trusting relationship.
4. Be prepared to "fire" some clients because they waste your time and provide low tangible and intangible rewards for you and their organization.
5. Strive to become a Level 3/Level 4 Trusted Advisor–Master Practitioner. Strive to be in the top 10% of consultants in terms of value delivered and value received.
6. Define your personal and professional purpose and connect with the clients that are like-minded. Use the Odyssey Arrow consistently to advance the relationship.
7. Design your business model and be able to describe it—who you are and what you do—on the back of a napkin.
8. Build your business with trust and integrity through talent-driven results and added defined value for the client.

My life, work, and experience in consulting has been and continues to be a journey, as the term "Odyssey" implies. We each approach consulting in our own way and to the beat of our own drum. Yes, the individuality of our expertise, approach, and application defines the consultant personality, business model, and brand. *The Business of Consulting* creates a consultant career path, with a proven client-focused methodology and process. Above all, it creates a community with consistent standards of practice, a set of common values, and a passion that will make a world of difference for each one of us and our clients.

Nothing Happens until Somebody Does Something

Art Boulay, CEO, Strategic Talent Management, Brunswick, Maine

I first heard John Butler speak in 2005 on "Odyssey: The Business of Consulting." John filled the room with his presence, and I was equally taken by his message. He pointed out that the difference between consultants making a million dollars a year and those making $50,000 a year is essentially … nothing. It is very much like a horse race where the first-place winner captures the lion's share of the winnings, and the rest of the top finishers share a fraction of the purse, even though they lose by a "nose." The real difference in financial results is in the hearts and minds of the consultants, the difference between a Level 3 or Level 4 Master Practitioner and a Level 1 or Level 2 Competent Warrior.

While the message was powerful, my income from consulting had started a serious upward trajectory in 2000, and by 2005, I was doing well financially. I felt I had no need to write a check to Odyssey or to any other program. This upward momentum continued through 2008, and I still did not consider signing up though I was aware of the program and trusted colleagues had completed Odyssey. Then came the economic collapse, and though 2009 was not a bad year financially, for the first time in nine years, my income went down instead of rising by double digits.

I signed up with Odyssey in November of 2009.

As you will note from my reflection so far, it was all about money. I thought Odyssey would help me get back on track with the income growth I had come to expect, and that the money train would continue. In the back of my mind, however, I knew there was more to this story than just money.

I began my consulting career in 1991 as a TQM consultant, and by 1993, I had "discovered" coaching. I really enjoyed it. I loved the interaction with my small-business clients. They were very bright technically, but they still benefited from my corporate management training, including TQM. During that time, Bill Maloney (my business partner) and I were introduced to assessments that were instrumental in my first wave of business growth. My business expanded, and I found myself doing more and more hiring selection work and relatively less coaching.

By the time 2008 rolled around, the majority of my income was from hiring selection, and all of the business growth was in that area. In fact, I was telling my business acquaintances that I was thinking of getting out of coaching altogether because it wasn't working. Coaching clients did not seem to want to follow up on their own commitments; they lacked focus, and I could not make any headway with them. Besides, the hiring selection business was going extremely well, until the economic crash.

In the fall of 2009, I put in calls to some of my best and longest-term clients and discovered that they were shrinking their operations. My biggest clients, on average, were shedding 60% of their staff. So, I decided that the problem was a lack of marketing ... Surely someone was hiring! I was shocked when 25% of my mailings came back as "undeliverable." That corresponded to clients and prospects who had already closed their doors or had downsized and moved. That marketing effort was a bust.

I talked to my colleagues who had been through Odyssey and read testimonials on the Odyssey website. At that time, most of the messages went along these lines: "Right after the program, I signed up a million-dollar client." But, my good friend, Greg Smith, told me his income had not increased at all. So I asked him if he thought I should sign up, and he said, "Absolutely yes! It will help blow the cobwebs out of your head." I thought I understood what Greg meant at the time, but it was only later that the true meaning of his recommendation sunk in. I signed up for Odyssey.

In Dublin, August 2010, I was working on my purpose statement to be delivered to my colleagues the next morning at the Odyssey MasterClass. I sat in front of a blank page for a couple of hours; my mind was as blank as the page before me. The task seemed impossibly difficult. And then I had a flash of inspiration and drew this on the flip chart page (Figure 7.1).

Then I wrote, "My purpose is to help others uncover their purpose." While I was sitting at my desk, I could hear John's voice in my head, talking about taking personal responsibility.

Right then, something clicked for me ... I needed to return to coaching. The reason my coaching clients were not following through on their

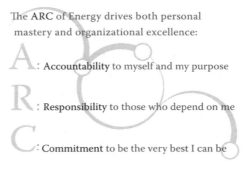

Figure 7.1   The Arc of Energy.

responsibilities, completing assignments, or making measurable progress was that I had let them off the hook. I hadn't made them follow through on their responsibilities. I let them off the hook because I had let myself off the hook. No matter what your role, manager, leader, coach, or parent, you cannot hold others accountable if you do not hold yourself accountable.

This was a major breakthrough for me, and I anticipated, once again, a fast-track return to financial rewards. It did not happen that way, however, because I was missing the other important lessons from John's 2005 speech and my 2010 experience on the Odyssey program. Winners do lots of things right, but the most important thing they have is the right mind-set. That mind-set includes

- Knowing your purpose
- Personal accountability
- Getting out of your own way (as John told me many times), and, most important of all
- Getting on with it

The latter has become my mantra, and when I find myself thinking through the solution, checking in with colleagues, signing up for another webinar, I can hear John telling me, "Get out of your own way, Boulay, and get on with it!"

The point is that in business, it is often more important to act than to get it exactly right. The fact is, we often get it wrong, but for every effort and failure, we learn something to make the next effort more successful and move our cause forward. If we only plan, think, and write about the future, we are not achieving the future. While planning and thinking can help avoid dumb mistakes, somebody had to build the first computer, launch the first rocket, or fly the first airplane. Nothing happens until somebody does something.

Since 2010, I have slowly improved my life by taking decisive actions in areas that appear to have little to do with business. I dropped 40 pounds and have maintained my ideal weight since 2011. I engaged a trainer and have been working out at least three hours a week since 2012. As a result, I have more energy and stamina. Significantly, I gained the self-confidence that comes from accomplishing difficult tasks. This led to small but significant changes in the way I talked about my business. I tell people about my own journey and the "Arc of Energy." I discuss my belief in goal achievement, which I call, "Achieve the Summit." The result is a palpable difference in my presence and authenticity when talking to a prospect or catching up with a client.

As the economy has revived, my coaching business has grown, and I have several clients at various levels in their careers, working on projects from mastering people management to planning for succession. Significantly, coaching clients own their success, and I do not have to try as hard to gain that ownership. This is exactly what I want to be doing. While the hiring selection business is coming back strongly, I advocate that larger companies and consultants engage me not so much to do the work but to enter a partnership to apply this knowledge to their business. This is a new aspect of my business, but in these many small ways, I am working closer to my purpose today than at any time in my consulting career.

I have also been more comfortable in seeking out others to whom I refer work or with whom I collaborate on areas that I do not do well, turning down business that does not interest me or engage my mind, respectfully declining to spend valuable time with people who are not authentic, and dropping vendors who do not measure up to my standards. Odyssey teaches us to be clear about our purpose, accept personal responsibility for our purpose, get out of our own way, and get on with it. I may be slower than some, but success is not an overnight process. Success sometimes looks like an "out of the blue" event, but there are many powerful examples of overnight successes that were decades in the making.

Success is not necessarily about dollars. Odyssey defines success as achieving your purpose. Do what you love, people will see and feel your passion and engage with you in a Level 3 or Level 4 partnership. The money may well follow in such an engagement, but the real winners are your heart and soul.

You are holding the book. You are ready to act. There is no better time than now. Get on with it.

Odyssey, the Rubicon, and Beyond

Carol Renaud Gaffney, PhD, Behavioral Intelligence Consultant® Integrated Behavioral Intelligence Solutions™ LLC, Barrington, Rhode Island

"Are you ready to cross the Rubicon?"

"I am."

With those words, in July 2007, symbolic and actual steps were taken into a new, uncharted, and exciting landscape.

The week leading up to that moment had been intense. I had listened to and learned from John and Imelda, as well as those in my cohort. I was heard, challenged, and given the opportunity to laugh, cry, talk, think, and spend uninterrupted time with myself. It had brought me to a point where I had established goals, understood barriers, and made decisions about my skills, creativity, value, and how I could contribute in my world of work.

My career has had a number of twists and turns. I started out in the emerging IT industry in the 1960s, went to psychology graduate school, became a psychologist health service provider, then a consultant and coach for high-performing teams and executives within a wide range of businesses.

My offering included a variety of options for performance improvement, but I soon learned that although I was providing good solutions, they were transactional in nature. Even though I was a creative and a global thinker, the different client services I offered were not organized within a comprehensive system. Neither my confidence in interacting with decision makers nor my ability to write effective value-based proposals were well developed. Although I had years of experience with people and organizations, I had not internalized the role of professional consultant.

The Odyssey process gave me the system for effective professional consulting. Odyssey ideas provided a new outlook for me on what to do to help clients make decisions and how to implement change.

I also realized that the consultant still brings himself or herself to each consulting situation. To be of exceptional value to clients, I wanted to bring a fresh perspective tailored to the client's culture and vision. It was also important to me that I wasn't simply a vehicle for the Odyssey process. I also needed to understand how I personally brought value to my clients.

During the year leading to the Odyssey interactive week, I had begun to develop Behavioral Intelligence, which is defined as "doing what's right to get the right things done."

By the end of the formal Odyssey meetings, when I said I was ready to cross the Rubicon, it was because I had crystallized the ideas for The STARR Process© (Stop, Think, Assess, Respond, Review) to improve Behavioral Intelligence, and I was prepared, with the Odyssey process understanding and materials, to approach and interact with clients more confidently, more holistically; with heart as well as hand, globally as well as functionally. It was also important for me that I had feedback from colleagues and knew that I would have friends and support on my journey.

I crossed the Rubicon in 2007. I have not retreated.
What have been long-term Odyssey results?

- Clear thinking
- Confidence in my value and my strengths
- A network of like-minded colleagues and collaborators
- An effective business consulting system adaptable to a variety of opportunities

Successful outcomes (meeting strategic goals) arise from the integration of a powerful consulting system (Odyssey) and a powerful system for improving business results and personal well-being (Behavioral Intelligence and the STARR process). The journey continues.

Changing Direction with Odyssey

Marcel van der Wal, Hermosillo, Mexico

2014 was quite a year for me. The decision to choose a different career path has been a life-changing experience.

Joining Odyssey: The Business of Consulting program has been a choice I will never regret, and nor do I regret my decision to change careers. At times, I need to use my strongest characteristics and personal drive for independence to keep me focused.

During the Odyssey process, I was able to collaborate with practicing consultants who have become my colleagues and a valued resource for me as I focus on finding Ideal Clients by using the Odyssey Arrow.

I am working hard to produce the best result possible and feel that the support given has been nothing but exceptional. We had our MasterClass in September 2014 in Ottawa, and my expectations were high. During these meetings, with Imelda and Shayne and the other Odyssey participants, my transformation process reached a new level.

I saw how the Odyssey process could work for me, and by applying the process, I can achieve extraordinary results. As my experience grows in the application of the Arrow, I can see how deviation from the process does not get results.

As a consultant looking at Levels 1–4 and targeting Level 4, it's obvious we never work on one level only. I need to be skilled enough at all levels, especially when starting out, to be able to generate revenue and to adapt quickly without losing a beat. Mastering the process is essential to building a sustainable business and is absolutely key to being successful as a consultant at a global level.

It's essential that I do exactly what I say I am going to do and do it when I say I am going to do it. Sounds simple, but it's the number one quality needed to build trust and credibility among your team and your clients.

In today's business environment, if you are committed to creating a meaningful impact with the work that you do as a consultant, you need to take the Odyssey process seriously. Why? One, we all have clients for whom we have to produce results, and two, when we act effectively as a consultant, we dramatically increase opportunities to produce results that are truly outstanding.

I have learned what makes a great consultant:

- Ask the right questions and listen intently. If you don't ask the right questions and listen to your client, you risk spending time and money on the wrong priorities.
- Establish great rapport with clients. You may have excellent ideas, but if you lack the savvy it takes to gain buy-in with stakeholders, then you fall flat.
- Understand the client's business. If you lack an understanding of the underlying business operations, you may try to bulldoze a solution that simply won't work.

In general, when you have clients, your ability to identify their needs and implement the right solution is critical to success, but it's not everything, and it's definitely not sufficient to make you a great consultant. Your positive mind-set and presence are also vital.

I am grateful that I chose the Odyssey process as my guide to success. I am convinced it has been the right choice. With that also comes a great sense of gratitude for being coached and mentored by someone I truly have come to love and respect—my coach, Dr. Shayne Tracy. For anyone even remotely thinking of entering the field of consulting or updating their consulting skills, Odyssey is the way to go. I have met great people, including Imelda, and am very grateful to everyone who's been involved in my transformation.

Odyssey Helped Me to See Myself through the Fog

Andrew Yoshioka, Sanbonki Inc., Ontario, Canada

During my last corporate job in 2009, I met Dr. Shayne Tracy. He had been retained by my company to benchmark management and workforce. As part of that process, he assessed me and the job I was doing. When we reviewed what he had found, he pointed out an obvious conflict between who I was and the work that I did. This wasn't really news to me. I just assumed everyone grumbled about their work and that I was no different. Thinking about it later, however, it occurred to me that during my career, I had missed a number of signals that should have lead me to realize that I should run my own business.

When my company priorities changed, I left with a severance package and embarked on bucket list travels to see the world and to discover the secrets of wealth and happiness. (Ha!) When I came home, I kept getting referrals from people who needed help getting their businesses off the ground. I had no idea about Ideal Clients at the time. I was just convinced I could solve their challenges. However, these assignments usually collapsed due to a lack of clarity around what success was, or what their expectations were, or about how long these ventures would take to get to market. I realized that there was something lacking in my consulting.

Around this time, Shayne suggested that if I was serious about consulting as a business, I should really consider Odyssey. I enrolled in the program, but frankly, I questioned my investment because though I was aware of the content, I still had no idea about my purpose or my plan—pretty much right up to travelling to the Odyssey MasterClass. The small group session, however, brought about a personal epiphany. I realized that I needed to abandon some of the things in my life that had been holding me back. This was such a relief. I came home from the trip finally seeing my new self through the fog on the road ahead. I knew I was heading in the right direction.

It has taken some time, and I have pivoted the business several times, but repeat assignments are coming regularly now, from clients who trust and value my solutions.

Further iteration of my value proposition took a while to develop. I needed a statement that captured what I do and also validated the needs of and opportunities faced by our clients. I eventually settled on this: "We position businesses for investment, partnerships, and value growth." It seemed to cover the themes that arose consistently: The need for development capital, finding partners, and alliances (development/distribution/sales chan-nels) and growing the client's business value (new segments/higher value/productivity).

Today, my business is not about repeated, mundane transactional tasks like writing business plans. Instead, I am a Trusted Advisor to the client. We provide insight to customer segmentation or help translate good ideas into technologies that are correctly positioned. We try to overcome the client's tendency to build a "field of dreams" where it is left to the customer to fig-ure out what it is and why they need it. You become the sculptor. You take a raw slab and deliver to your client the image of success they have in their head but which they struggle to articulate.

I now donate some of my time working with start-ups and organize networking functions in my industry. Donating my time as a volunteer has confirmed for me that I do add value. It has also opened many doors in expanding my network beyond the immediate circle of former corporate world contacts. Others are now championing my brand.

In February 2014, I received recognition for my impact, with the Life Sciences Ontario Volunteer of the Year Award. That accolade accelerated my business development through all the early steps of validation because the referral trusts the opinion of your mutual gatekeeper. Finding the connectors and even becoming one of the connectors has been an important steps in the process.

Your client depends on you to find the solution for them. They have no interest in hearing you whine about the hoops you may need to jump through to do it. One lesson I recall from Odyssey is that you should project your business to appear bigger than you really are, but not in a mislead-ing way. Several times, I have got together with a network of colleagues to engage projects that were beyond our individual areas of scope. We have expanded into other business categories and shared the revenues of projects that we might not have landed on our own. Clients in knowledge businesses may think their problem is technical, but it is usually a business problem.

Your client just wants the solution.

In Conclusion

We thank our Odyssey graduates who contributed their reflections to this chapter and to those who so generously shared their experiences in the "Odyssey in Action" sections throughout the book. These consultants, who work at the highest levels of their profession right around the world, endorse the practical results made possible by integrating Odyssey concepts into their consulting businesses. As they have testified, Odyssey processes and programs have had a transformational influence on their personal and working lives. If you would like to talk about participating in Odyssey, our contact details are listed in the coming pages.

Wishing you masterful consulting and success in your life and business.

Imelda K. Butler
Dr. Shayne Tracy

About Odyssey Consulting Institute

Our Mission Statement

We partner with our clients to create corporate strategic advantage by embedding innovative thought work, strategies, and systems to help transform cultural, strategic, and human capital.

A Word about the Programs We Offer

Odyssey Consulting Institute™, through Odyssey: The Business of Consulting™, offers consultants the opportunity to partake in a journey to become leading edge practitioners. You will

- Advance from being a competent consultant to becoming a respected Master Practitioner in your profession;
- Apply proven business and professional strategies to maximize your rewards;
- Collaborate on global corporate opportunities;
- Maximize your return on investment;
- Fulfil your true purpose and serve your clients in a strategic, results-based forum;
- Develop a consulting business model that works for you and your clients;
- Learn the business of consulting systems, processes, and methodologies for success.

Odyssey Competent Consultant™

This process is comprised of a webinar series together with individualized coaching and mentoring. It provides participants with the toolkit for becoming a competent consultant and attaining personal and professional success.

Odyssey Transformational MasterClass™

This transformational process, facilitated by Odyssey Master Practitioners™, embraces success and fulfilment. The Odyssey Transformational MasterClass™ brings clarity and direction to life, business purpose, and destiny. Graduates receive certification and membership of the Odyssey Alumni™ and join an elite network of fellow, purpose-driven professionals.

Odyssey Trusted Advisor™

The Odyssey Trusted Advisor™ advanced consultant process is comprised of the advanced webinar and individualized coaching and mentoring series. The process is designed to facilitate participants in being successful at higher personal and business levels.

Contact

Imelda K. Butler, Chairperson
Odyssey Consulting Institute™
Phone: 353 45 899748
Imeldabutler@OdysseyConsultingInstitute.com
Skype: imeldabutler
Dr. Shayne Tracy, Director
Odyssey Consulting Institute™
Drtracy@OdysseyConsultingInstitute.com
Phone: 001 416 7370407
Skype: Shayne.Tracy
www.odysseyconsultinginstitute.com

Index

Page numbers ending in "f" refer to figures. Page numbers ending in "t" refer to tables.

About the Authors

Imelda K. Butler is a global corporate thought leader for Odyssey Consulting Institute™, where she is also the chairperson, and for Odyssey The Business of Consulting™. She is also the managing director of Century Management Ltd. She inspires, energizes, influences, and facilitates consultants to become the very best they can be, by identifying, clarifying, and focusing on their purpose, passion, and talents in life and business, all while integrating the proven success system and methodology of the Odyssey process.

Imelda and her husband John, who sadly passed away suddenly in 2010, created the Odyssey concept and methodology based on their twenty-five year partnership in their consulting business. During that time, they saw many consultants leaving business on the table and working at low levels within the profession.

John and Imelda, and their good friend Dave Bonnstetter, CEO of Success Insights International, set up Odyssey: The Business of Consulting™ in 2005 with the vision to create the premier consulting organization and to guide consultants in the creation of leading-edge consulting businesses around the globe.

This was the motivation behind creating a powerful series of world-class business consulting concepts and methodologies to help consultants build, grow, and transform their consulting businesses.

By applying Odyssey methodologies and interventions, consultants integrate and implement a proven worldwide success system into their client assignments.

Imelda is passionate about maximizing human potential and living your life fully, so you don't go to the grave with your music still in you. She is an advocate for business and personal success, whatever your field of endeavor.

She is also the managing director of Century Management, a consulting business that she and John set up in 1989. In this role, she specializes in strategic change management processes and systems, enabling organizations to achieve and maintain competitive business advantage.

She currently works as a strategic partner with some of Ireland's most successful and prestigious organizations. She partners with key stakeholders in realizing client organizations' full potential by developing their culture, vision, strategic direction, and human capital. Imelda has extensive experience in individual, team, and organization development.

Since 1992, Imelda and Century Management have been the master distributor in Ireland for TTI Success Insights International's competency, benchmarking, measurement, personal talent, behaviors, motivators, and emotional intelligence portfolio of assessments.

Imelda is a fellow of the Institute of Management Consultants in Ireland, holds an honors degree in Management and a diploma in Theology and Relationship Facilitation.

A native of County Wicklow, Imelda lives in the beautiful countryside of Forenaughts, County Kildare, where she is involved in local community organizations. She enjoys her leisure time in the company of her two beautiful daughters, Michelle and Maria, and their husbands, Patrick and Geoffrey. She has one awesome grandchild, with another on the way. She likes to walk in the country, relax with friends, and read spiritual, inspirational, and business books.

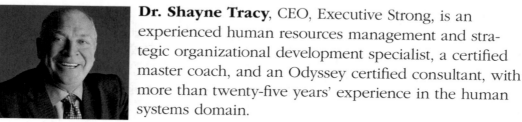 **Dr. Shayne Tracy**, CEO, Executive Strong, is an experienced human resources management and strategic organizational development specialist, a certified master coach, and an Odyssey certified consultant, with more than twenty-five years' experience in the human systems domain.

He provides advice, processes, methodologies, and experiences for senior management and organizations to create or enhance tangible asset value through improved performance, productivity, and profitability. He divides his time between consulting, executive coaching, and master coach and consultant certification.

Dr. Tracy began his career in education as a teacher, before becoming an education administrator and then taking on a senior role in human resources with one of the largest public school boards in Canada.

He left the public sector when the first PC hit the first desk and founded Human Resources Technologies in the mid-1980s to develop human resources and training information systems. The company subsequently installed more than 400 systems in small, medium, and large organizations across Canada. Shayne's vision was to provide human resources technology solutions to companies to enable practitioners to spend more time on operational and strategic involvement with "the people … who are your business."

Answering his Odyssey calling ten years later, Shayne embarked on a consulting career with a vision to assist individuals and organizations in making the changes required to get them where they want to go. He has consulted to a wide range of private and public organizations, both local and international, and in sectors which include hi-tech, manufacturing, service, and retail.

He says, "All companies, no matter what they produce or what services they provide, have the challenges of constant change and growth … or decline. The key variables that determine growth are leadership, management, employee engagement, and the value-based remuneration of their people, who work with the right motivators, skills, behavior, emotional intelligence, and measured results."

Shayne is a director of the Odyssey Consulting Institute™ where he provides coaching and cofacilitates the Odyssey MasterClass™.

He believes that Odyssey: The Business of Consulting is the boot camp for people who want to be consultants, or those in consulting who aspire to achieve their purpose and to be the best consultants they can be by making a difference in organizations and in the world.

Shayne lives in Mississauga, Ontario, Canada, with his wife Mary. They have three wonderful daughters and nine amazing grandchildren.